To my amazing husband Steve,

I can't even imagine doing this life without you. You inspire, believe in and strengthen me. You are my husband, best friend and greatest encourager. Thank you for the example you set in loving people, serving others and leading well. You help me and our beautiful children navigate the 'Now What?' moments of life with such trust and strength in God.

I have never seen you doubt, quit or waver in your relentless faith. You can find the rainbows in the rainstorms and make the bitter taste sweet.

So grateful you embrace 'crazy' with me.

I love you.

Forever

Charl xxx

Now What?

Charlotte Gambill

Believes Books Ltd

BELIEVES BOOKS LIMITED

35 WESTGATE

HUDDERSFIELD

WEST YORKSHIRE

HD1 1PA

With thanks to Hannah Jowett who provided editorial and copywriting services Email: hannahjowett@gmail.com

British Library Cataloguing in Publication Data. A catalogue record for this book is available from the British Library.

ISBN 978-0-9568564-1-8

Contents

Now
what?

"You were born to leave your footprints on the mountain tops, to carve new paths through your valleys and to discover hidden treasures in the trials you face."

Chapter 1

Now What?

'Somebody call me a taxi! I'm a lost preacher and I'm late for church!' I had just run into a bar looking disheveled and visibly upset, to be met with bemused looks from a room full of afternoon drinkers. By their response I could tell that my grand entrance was an unusual turn of events. Not only had a crazy English woman looking like she had just run a marathon interrupted them, I had no idea where I was and even less idea of where I was going. I had set off for a run from where I was staying and got totally lost. I had no mobile phone to call anyone and no money to pay for the taxi they called me. I was left trying to persuade the driver to take me on a scenic tour of the neighbourhood to help me find my way home. To make matters worse, the meeting I was scheduled to preach at was due to start in just 30 minutes. I was left panicking and completely lost thinking, 'Now What?'

The day had started well and nothing about it gave me any clues as to the confusion that lay moments ahead. It was a hot summer's day in California, I was staying with friends and was due to speak at their church services that evening, all five of them. I decided to get some fresh air first by venturing out for a quick jog around the neighbourhood with my husband, Steve.

Our friends suggested a good running route and gave us a printed map with handwritten instructions on it to help us find our way. We set off enthusiastically but after about 15 minutes running under the hot sun we decided it was time to pick up the pace and head back. We chose to split up so that I could get back quickly and make my final preparations to preach. I have never been a great map reader so we tore the instructions in half, I took the written directions and left Steve with the map. I thought, 'how hard could it be to follow a few left and right turns?' But this was the first in a line of very bad decisions that I was about to make.

After running flat out for another 30 minutes, I began to realise that something was seriously wrong. The short route I was supposed to be running seemed more like a marathon. I found myself out of breath and approaching the entrance to a freeway which even I knew was not an option to run down.

I stopped and looked around me for something familiar but I couldn't see any landmarks that I recognised. I was disorientated, exhausted and completely at a loss as to what to do next. I started to panic as I shouted out in frustration 'Now What?'

This was how I had ended up dashing into a bar to ask for directions and it was why I was now in the back of a taxi with no money to pay the driver. We drove around the area looking for anything I might recognise and after several wrong turns, I finally caught sight of a familiar road sign and then saw Steve who was just returning from his run. I was overwhelmed with relief and my panic began to subside.

Careless Confusion

When I talked to my friends afterwards, it became evident that a small but very important left turn had been omitted from the directions I was given. It wasn't a deliberate plan they had hatched to sabotage my afternoon run or to confuse me. My 'Now What?' moment was caused by a simple, careless mistake. It was made worse by my own failure to prepare for my jog in an unfamiliar place, I hadn't even taken the address of where I was staying with me. My crisis was the result of carelessness and complacency and I was caught completely off guard.

I have thought about my run many times and recalled how I felt on that day - disoriented, confused and completely panicked. I suddenly found myself in a situation that I hadn't seen coming and had no plan to get out of. All I could do was use my initiative, desperately look for a solution, trust strangers and pray that I would somehow find my way home.

We all experience these moments where we end up feeling disoriented and lost in life and end up thinking 'Now What?' They can be caused by many different things, from our own mistakes to other people's carelessness at times. 'Now What?' moments can be a disappointment, a family tragedy, a redundancy, marriage break up or business failure that you weren't expecting. They can be caused when an answer to prayer is delayed or when a dream you had appears to be impossible to reach. 'Now What?' moments are the unexpected challenges that can leave us feeling bewildered and unsure of which way to turn. We all have to journey through them and find answers to the difficult questions of what to do, say or even pray.

Faith Fractures

I remember years ago when we were house hunting, we found a beautiful home that seemed like the ideal next step for our family. Everything about it looked great, from the location to the decoration. We were negotiating to buy the house when the structural survey came back. It showed that the house had major foundational problems that weakened the structure. It looked fine on the outside, but over the years the pressure placed on the foundations would eventually cause cracks in the house. This fault would eventually cause the house to become a place of danger and harm instead of being the safe home we desired.

In a similar way, our 'Now What?' moments can be like having a structural survey carried out on our lives. They reveal what's beneath the well-decorated frontage of our faith and peel away the layers of paint we have covered our lives in to hide our faults instead of fixing them. The pressure they place on us can highlight hairline cracks in our convictions and reveal fractures in our faith. Uncomfortable as it sounds, I believe we need to embrace 'Now What?' moments and be grateful for the way they can test us. Sometimes we can think we have unshakeable faith until the shaking begins. We think our belief is strong until we face illness, or that our love is solid until it is tested by betrayal.

If you want to build a difference-making life, you need to make sure it can withstand even the most violent of storms. I would certainly prefer to be made aware of any fault lines in my life so that I can fix them, rather than have my life collapse later on. When a building has a structural fault, it can be underpinned to help strengthen it. We need to underpin our life with God's truth to keep us upright and strengthen our foundations so that we can stay standing through our 'Now What?' moment.

Marred or Marked

God didn't destine you to be marked by life, but to make a mark on life. You were born to leave your footprints on the mountaintops, to carve new paths through your valleys and to discover hidden treasure in the trials you may face. He created you to be an overcomer, victorious, His beloved and someone who would make a mark on history. The enemy knows the incredible potential that is in your life, so from the very beginning he has sought to prevent you from making your mark. His aim is to hinder your progress and prevent you from reaching the heights you can discover. He doesn't want your life to be marked for greatness, he wants it to be marred.

The word mar means to mark in a disfiguring manner and I believe the enemy wants to mar our lives through the 'Now What?' moments we face. He wants to disfigure our view of God to scar our spirit and leave us marred by our circumstances.

When we face 'Now What?' moments, the way we respond to them can cause us to either leave a mark, or to be marred. I want to take some time to look at the life of one man who failed to negotiate his moment and consequently ended up disfiguring and damaging his life.

As the firstborn son of Adam and Eve, Cain was someone who was gifted with the amazing opportunity to leave a distinctive and special mark on the world. He was destined to be a history maker and to set the bar for the generations who would come after him. Yet Cain allowed feelings of jealousy and bitterness to mar his spirit and his behaviour became driven by his warped and disfigured thinking. (Genesis 4:2-15)

Cain grew crops and his younger brother, Abel, kept flocks. It was time for the brothers to make an offering to God. It was an opportunity for them to make a mark and demonstrate their devotion to God by giving the very best of their crops and flocks as an act of worship. But in this mark-making moment Cain gave an offering that was disfigured and blemished, while Abel brought his best. When God spoke to Cain about the lesser offering he had given, he responded in a way that would mar his life forever.

Cain was very angry and his face was downcast. Then the Lord said to Cain, "Why are you angry and why is your face downcast? If you do what is right, will you not be accepted? But if you do not do what is right, sin is crouching at your door, and it desires to have you. But you must master it." (Genesis 4:5-7)

Like Cain, in 'Now What?' moments you will find yourself faced with the choice to do right, or to do wrong. You get to choose your attitude and your actions. Cain allowed his own feelings of jealousy and pride to mar his attitude towards his brother and become disfigured by anger and rage. Sin was crouching at his door ready to scar his spirit and alter his destiny, and Cain invited it in.

A Disfigured Destiny

What happened next was tragic. 'Now Cain said to his brother Abel, "Hey, let's go out to the field." And while they were in the field Cain attacked his brother Abel, and he killed him. Then the Lord said to Cain, "Where is your brother Abel?" "I don't know." he replied. "Am I my brother's keeper?"' (Genesis 4:8-9)

There is a well known saying which describes what happened next, 'hurt people, hurt people!' The fact is when our lives are disfigured we often go on to damage others. If our lives become marred by 'Now What?' moments the fall out can affect many more people than just ourselves. God intended for Cain and Abel to encourage and support one another and to be each others keepers. Instead, their relationship was destroyed and Cain's disfigurement cost Abel his life.

There are many examples of marred and disfigured lives causing damage to others. Joseph's dream caused his brothers to be marred by jealousy and they threw him into a pit and then sold him into slavery. Saul was marred by bitterness about David's success in battle, so he set out to destroy him. From the beginning of time, 'Now What?' moments have been used by the enemy to divide families and separate friends. If we learn to navigate them in the right way we can avoid leaving a trail of damaged relationships behind us. When we are tested we need to keep focused on what really matters in life. We must find a way to move beyond the situations that could mar us so we don't end up losing our way like Cain.

A Restless Wanderer

'The Lord said to Cain, "What have you done? Listen! Your brother's blood cries out to me from the ground. Now you are under a curse and driven from the ground which opened its mouth to receive your brother's blood from your hand. When you work the ground it will no longer yield its crops for you. You will be a restless wanderer on the earth." Cain said to the Lord, "My punishment is more than I can bear. Today you are driving me from the land and I will be hidden from your presence. I will be a restless wanderer on the earth and whoever finds me will kill me." But the Lord said to him, "Not so; if anyone kills Cain he will suffer vengeance seven times over." Then the Lord put a mark on Cain so that no-one who found him would kill him. So Cain went out from the Lord's presence and he lived in the land of Nod. '(Genesis 4:9-15)

Our failure to navigate our own testing will ultimately cause us to become disorientated in our own destiny. Like Cain, we can end up being a restless wanderer in the land of Nod. This picture is such a prophetic statement of what happens if we allow our feelings to shape our future. We need to keep our emotions in check so they don't drive us to act in a reckless or rebellious way. I have seen many people react badly and lose their sense of purpose during 'Now What?' moments. Before the trial hit, they were firm in their convictions, but they allowed the experience to harden their hearts and weaken their commitment.

Marred people do not make a mark on life and sadly, their disfigurement can affect many others. For example, have you ever heard of Irad, Mehujael, Lamech, Zillah, Adah or Jabal? They all came from the lineage of Cain. None of them made a mark on life. The family even went on to mar each other and became known for murder and incest. They also became restless wanderers, asleep to their potential as they grew up in the aptly named land of Nod. If we want to leave a positive legacy for those who will follow us, we need to understand that our ability to overcome the challenges we face will become others inheritance.

In this book, I want to offer some thoughts that have helped me to navigate these moments. They have allowed me to stay consistent in the face of confusion, advance instead of retreat and to find purpose in the pain.

I pray as you read this book you would begin to see that every 'Now What?' moment you face is also an opportunity to shape history. I pray you will awaken to the truth that the situation you may be struggling with right now can become part of your testimony. Cain failed to turn his test into a triumph, but we can choose to respond differently. David didn't allow Saul's bitterness to disfigure him. He rose above the opposition and became a man after Gods own heart. Joseph didn't allow his brothers' betrayal or his false imprisonment to mar him and he became Prime Minister, saving a generation from famine. We need to see that what makes the difference isn't down to the circumstances, but to our response.

I pray you will refuse to be marred and will commit to making your mark. You were born to live a remarkable life, so don't settle for anything less. Keep on moving, embrace every 'Now What?' challenge and use them to build a faith without fractures.

Now What?

Tips For Navigating 'Now What?' Moments

1. 'Now What?' moments visit everyones life. You are not alone.

2. Don't wait for the crisis to reveal your cracks.

3. We must decide not to be marred, but make our mark.

4. Failure to navigate our 'Now What?' can derail our destiny.

5. You were born to be remarkable, don't let circumstances tell you differently.

"We need to learn to use our spiritual gear shift to balance the force we should apply with the speed at which we wish to travel."

Chapter 2

Grinding Gears

Being married to an American has many great advantages. Steve and I have always loved the mix of traditions and celebrations that it brings to our family. Yet when we met, one thing we didn't love was each others way of driving. Firstly, we had learnt to drive on opposite sides of the road and the rules are very different between the UK and the US. For example, in America you are allowed to turn right at a red traffic light. When Steve moved to the UK he quickly found out the hard way that this is most definitely not okay! He also had to negotiate roundabouts for the first time which are very different to four-way stops in America. As you can imagine, these differences made for some fairly interesting and a few life threatening adventures.

Yet for many of my American friends who visit the UK, what baffles them the most is having to drive a car with a manual gearbox, or stick shift as they call it over there. Most of them learned to drive in an automatic so they aren't as used to a stick shift.

I will never forget one of the first dates I went on with Steve. He had come over to study in England for a year and had bought a very old stick shift car on his very limited student budget. He picked me up in this red, beat up old car and as we set off his nerves were very apparent. He had to drive on what was to him, the wrong side of the road and had the added challenge of having to negotiate narrow country lanes when he was used to wide-open freeways. He kept driving down the middle of the lanes and I had to remind him he wasn't on a one-way system, there would be traffic coming the other way. I remember at one point he struggled to navigate a roundabout and ended up driving straight over it instead of around it. Having me screaming with fear in the passenger seat didn't make for the most romantic start to our evening. As an added pressure the car was a stick shift and he struggled with changing gears for the entire journey because he was so used to driving an automatic. The car kept jolting as he tried to make a smooth transition between the gears, and there was an awful grinding sound coming from the gearbox when he didn't get it right.

Automatic or Manual?

When we come to Christ we can think it means our lives move from manual to automatic mode. We can wrongly believe that now we belong to God, we can sit back as a passenger while he drives the vehicle for us. In our 'Now What?' moments we can talk to God about our struggles as if it's his job to change gear without us being involved.

I have come to realise that when we decide to follow Christ we don't trade our manual self-drive life for an automatic, it's the other way around. Let me explain what I mean. Before we knew Christ we lived a life that was inwardly focused. We were our own main priority, so the decisions we made were often self-centred. We felt no need to drive in a way that would take God's purpose for our lives into account, or to follow his spiritual highway code to forgive others and to love and serve him. We didn't have to change gear, slow down to help someone else, or feel the need to use reverse to turn around when we sinned. We were driving our lives on automatic.

However, when we give our lives to Him, God becomes our internal driving instructor. When we surrendered our will to Him, the car of our life was adapted and we gained a spiritual stick shift called the Holy Spirit. He came into our life to make us more sensitive to the gears God has for our journey. The Bible says, 'Since we live by the Spirit, let us keep in step with the Spirit.' (Galatians 5:25) To keep in step with someone, you have to be able to change your speed to match their pace. In other words you could say that we have to learn how to change gear ourselves. We can no longer drive on automatic but must learn to use different spiritual gears that allow us to stay in sync with God. Otherwise we will start to grind spiritually and will be unable to make smooth transitions in our 'Now What?' moments. Most experienced drivers will tell you they love to use gears because it makes driving more interactive and fun. God wants you to have an interactive destiny, so you must learn to use each gear and become competent at driving across all kinds of terrain.

The Gear Shift

Gears work by balancing two factors, force and speed. The amount of power needed in each gear differs as does the amount of control. The same is true in life, we need to learn to balance the force we apply in various situations and control the speed at which we try to get things done. If we are always driving at top speed and have no control we are in trouble. But if we have too much control and no momentum we will grind to a sudden halt. To navigate life and all its challenges we need both.

Each gear requires a different balance of power and control according to the purpose it is destined to perform. For example, first gear is for getting started. It provides enough energy for the car to get moving and engage. The main purpose of second gear is for manoeuvring around obstacles. Third gear is most useful when you are climbing up a hill or rough terrain. Then as the road levels out and the landscape widens you can move into fourth and fifth gears and drive faster.

I have found my 'Now What?' moments have required me to use different gears to negotiate the challenges I faced. Sometimes I have needed to make a first gear decision and start something new. It has meant slowing down long enough for me to acquire control of the situation I face and then applying enough power to gain momentum. Other times I have needed to use second gear to enable me to manoeuvre around people, to navigate differences and avoid collisions. Other times I have needed enough speed to climb a hill or for a long distance drive.

There is also a need for a gear called reverse. Too often we have viewed this gear negatively because we think that going backwards is the wrong direction and that it will hinder our momentum in life. Yet, I have found that this isn't always true.

Although reverse is unsuitable for long distances and it will lead to an accident if you use it on the freeway, there are times when we all need to back up. If in your 'Now What?' moment you've taken a wrong turn, you may need your reverse gear. Perhaps the stress of your circumstance has caused you to speak rashly or make panic decisions and you need to back up and put things right. If it wasn't for the reverse gear, the prodigal son would have never come home and maybe you need the grace of that gear to find your way back too. Every gear has a specific purpose and once we learn to engage them at the right time, we can continue our journey with greater maturity and fewer casualties.

A Need for Speed

We live in an instant world where speed is highly valued. We want fast food, microwave meals, faster service, and instant access. This expectation that everything should happen quickly can make us impatient in our walk with God. We can end up ignoring the starter gears and be in a rush to reach fifth so we can maximise our speed and go faster for longer. We long to find that stretch of spiritual road that has no speed limit so we can hit cruise control and just race ahead.

I am all for going faster and I believe that momentum is a key to us building and growing the things of God, but we would be foolish to think life is about living at a breakneck speed. In reality, there is no road that will allow you to stay in fifth gear. Even if you are on the German autobahns where there's no speed limit, eventually you will have to slow down for something called traffic! There will be obstacles coming up on the horizon that you will have to navigate. Someone's going to break down, there's going to be a diversion or road works outside of your planning that will interrupt your journey. If we don't allow for these situations we will guarantee a collision in our future and the potential death of passengers and dreams. Our ability to use our spiritual gear shift is what will help us avoid those obstacles and navigate other people's traffic in 'Now What?' moments.

So ask yourself, 'am I in the right gear? Am I in the right gear in my thinking, in my praying and in my expectation? Am I in a gear that's going to help me through this stage of my journey?' God wants us to have the ability to find the right internal gear. We shouldn't stall every time we face a 'Now What?' moment but we need the wisdom to simply adjust our gears to the different types of roads we find ourselves driving on.

Lesson From the Master

Jesus was an expert driver when it came to gears. He never put His life into automatic mode but would constantly adapt and adjust His speed to suit the people He came to reach. He slowed down to pick up the broken and let others get on board. At other times He would move quickly to bring miracles and deliverance to those waiting. Jesus didn't grind His way through different circumstances, He knew how to make each transition.

Jesus also could transition from the euphoria of a fifth gear moment when the crowd were shouting "Hosanna, hosanna," into reverse when the same crowd shouted "crucify Him, crucify Him." He always knew the appropriate speed for the situation He faced and the people He was with. He knew how to navigate the 'Now What?' moments when those around

Him stalled. He knew which gear was needed to navigate Judas' betrayal and Peter's gear grinding denial.

I love how Jesus became a driving instructor to His team. When they stalled He helped them get moving again. After Peter stalled and denied Him, Jesus returned to the site of His breakdown to help Peter jump start his destiny and get back on the road he was called to travel.

The Bible says, 'When they had finished eating, Jesus said to Simon Peter, "Simon son of John, do you love me more than these?"
"Yes, Lord," he said, "you know that I love you."
Jesus said, "Feed my lambs."
Again Jesus said, "Simon son of John, do you love me?"
He answered, "Yes, Lord, you know that I love you."
Jesus said, "Take care of my sheep."
The third time he said to him, "Simon son of John, do you love me?"
Peter was hurt because Jesus asked him the third time, "Do you love me?" He said, "Lord, you know all things; you know that I love you."
Jesus said, "Feed my sheep."' (John 21:15-17)

As Jesus spoke words of affirmation over him at the waters edge, He was helping Peter change gears. It was as if with every response he made, Peter was turning the key in the ignition of his life until his conviction sparked and the engine of his life roared back into motion.

Fifth Gear Prophet

Elijah was a prophet that knew all about using fifth gear. He often did life at breakneck speed; in the space of one day he experienced the adrenalin rush of calling down fire and ran so fast he outpaced a chariot. (1 Kings 18) So when one chapter later we read about him lying under a tree with his life at a standstill, praying that God would take his life, it's a bit alarming.

Elijah suddenly found himself fearing for his life when Queen Jezebel decided she wanted him dead in revenge for him slaying the prophets of Baal. This news caught him unprepared and he was unable to change gears to navigate a way through the circumstance. He set off in the opposite direction at his usual high speed pace until he ran out of fuel. Elijah allowed negativity to take control of the steering wheel of his life and he veered quickly off course. He rapidly went from having his accelerator flat to the floor for God to an emergency stop that left him feeling suicidal. (1 Kings 19)

'Now What?' moments can cause pressure points in our lives and if we don't handle them well we can end up making bad choices and doing things that are out of character. Elijah certainly didn't appear to be someone who was prone to bouts of depression, he was a mighty prophet and faithful servant of God who had performed incredible miracles. Yet, he ended up feeling so beaten by his circumstances that he allowed his feelings to reroute his life from the road he should have been on.

As a church leader I have seen many people reroute their life following 'Now What?' moments. Often they were people who were very active in the life of the church and they seemed to just fade away. You are left wondering what on earth happened to them. I think many simply hit a circumstance or problem that stalled their engine spiritually. It stole their momentum and they allowed it to drain every drop of faith from the petrol tank of their life. After that they struggled to restart their engine and get moving again. For others it could be that they were driving so fast, they were reckless and lost control and injured themselves and other innocent travellers.

Often, when people crash who are in ministry they find it so hard to recover. It means admitting they were out of control and having to start again. Many don't want to return to the scene of the accident because they are too embarrassed to face the eye-witnesses. They feel guilty that their dangerous driving caused a collision. We need to show grace when we see someone who has come off the road because we all make mistakes at times and need refresher courses to improve our driving skills. We don't want to lose any more good people due to accidents. When we find those who have come off the road and ended up in a ditch we need to encourage them to get back in the drivers seat, just as God did with Elijah. His last days could have been spent languishing under a tree in self-pity, but fortunately his journey wasn't over.

Driving School

Elijah was sat parked up, with his gear stick in neutral, when God appeared to give him a valuable lesson in how to change gears. He said, 'What are you doing here Elijah?' The prophet explained how he had been on full throttle in fifth gear for the Lord, and had now come to an abrupt and unexpected halt.

'He said, "I've been so very zealous for the Lord God Almighty. The Israelites have rejected your covenant, they've broken down your altars and put your prophets to death with the sword. I'm the only one left and now they are trying to kill me too."' (1 Kings 19:9-10)

The Lord said to him, 'OK, we're going to go back to driving school. Get the engine of your life onto that mountain because I'm going to teach you something.'

So Elijah stood at the edge of the mountain and I love how God begins to minister to him and help him. He begins by sending him a fifth gear wind, a powerful fast-moving force of nature that rushed by. Elijah was comfortable around the God of the supernatural and he was used to seeing signs and wonders. As the wind shattered the rocks around him Elijah probably thought God was going to do something miraculous to solve his problems, but nothing happened. God was using the wind to teach him he didn't just use fifth gear. Next came a fourth gear earthquake, but the Lord wasn't in the earthquake either. Then a third gear fire arrived, but the Lord wasn't in the fire. And after the fire came a very gentle first gear whisper. It was as if God was moving down gears one at a time until he had Elijah's full attention. He knew that if Elijah's stalled life was to be jump-started he needed to be in first gear to get moving again.

As Elijah leaned in and listened to God whisper, it re-fuelled the engine of his life. He knew it was time for him to move. It says, 'When Elijah heard it he pulled his cloak over his face and he went out and stood at the mouth of the cave. Then the voice said to him, "What are you doing here Elijah?"' (1 Kings 19:11)

In our 'Now What?' moments, God will often seek us out because there are things that he wants to speak into our lives. Often he finds us in a similar place to Elijah, feeling defeated, confused and wondering what the future holds. He understands that in these times we need first gear. He isn't abrupt, in His grace He approaches us in the right gear for the situation we find ourselves in.

'Again, God asked Elijah, "What are you doing here?" Elijah again responded "I've been zealous for the Lord God Almighty. The Israelites have rejected your covenants, destroyed your altars, and put your prophets to death with the sword. And I am the only one left and now they are trying to kill me too." And the Lord said to him, "Go back the way you came."' It was time for Elijah to put his gear stick in reverse. (1 Kings 19:15)

For Elijah, finding reverse was not about going back to his past, it was about going back the way he came to reconnect with his future and destiny. It was about driving on familiar roads, this time with a better understanding of how to change gear at the right moment. Maybe he had even zoomed past the very person God had lined up to carry His anointing. This time he demonstrated his new driving skills and swapped his accelerator for the brake to make a destiny-defining connection.

Elijah was instructed to slow down and reverse. He had to go back the way he came to fulfill his destiny, to anoint kings and to mentor his successor, Elisha.

Pit Stop

We must all allow God to wave the pit stop flag in our lives. In Formula One races, teams flag their drivers down and get them to leave the race temporarily for a pit stop while they change tyres and refuel. We also need to be alert and respond to the Holy Spirit flagging us down for essential maintenance. If you feel you are in a position to win the race, being flagged in can feel like an unnecessary interruption that could mean we end up wasting time and getting behind. We need to see that God's pit stops are vital if we want to finish the race.

I remember one time being extremely busy with a project I had embarked upon. It seemed to consume my every waking moment, from arriving at the office each day to the car ride home. Even in my down time the texts, questions and demands didn't stop. I complained to God about the situation and he directed the complaint back to me. I had been doing lap after lap and ignoring the Holy Spirit trying to flag me down for a pit stop. It was time for me to slow down, repent and learn how to accept the challenge without driving in a way that made me a danger on the roads. I had to start letting my own pit stop team help me to refuel and talk tactics about the next phase of the race. I had to prioritise my pit stops in the midst of my overwhelming desire to keep driving flat out. The word of God calls these moments 'selahs', they are a time to stop, pause, change gear and rethink the best route before you set off again.

It was amazing how my pit stops became my saving grace. I was reminded all over again to think about my driving style and not just tear past everyone in the name of Jesus!

I love how the story of the woman with the alabaster jar (Luke 7:37) describes what happens when we take a pit stop or selah moment. Those at the table were feasting and having fellowship when a woman entered who changed the whole atmosphere. She came in for a pit stop, fell at Jesus' feet and poured expensive perfume on him. She changed the pace of the party, moving it from a moment of feasting to a moment of honouring and worshipping her master. And while the disciples were complaining at the interruption, Jesus commended her as she had found the right gear in that moment. I often refer to that picture when life becomes busy and the guests, the food and the table can become more demanding than the reason why we are doing all this. I am reminded to transition down my gears until I slow down enough to sit at his feet. Then when I re-enter my race it will be for the right reasons and at the right pace.

My prayer is not just, 'Lord, let me get there', it's 'Lord, help me drive well'. I don't want to give my passengers whiplash as I grind gears and don't want to cause collisions by refusing to slow down and navigate obstacles. There are enough bad drivers on the roads already, let's not fill our spiritual roads with them too. I believe, 'Now What?' moments often require us to go back to driving school. They can teach us to plan pit stops into our journey and learn to transition and change our pace smoothly. If you feel your life has stalled, be strengthened. If you are stuck in the same gear go back to His feet and if you are running on empty stop to refuel. Let's learn in our 'Now What?' moments to use our gears without grinding.

Now What?

Tips For Changing Gear

1. Recognise your life needs gears spiritually to negotiate 'Now What?' moments.

2. Understand the purpose of each gear and when to use them.

3. In 'Now What?' moments, don't let fear take the wheel of your life.

4. Check if you are in the right gear in your thinking, praying and level of expectation.

5. If you stall the engine of your life don't quit! God can get you going again.

"'Now What?' moments can distort our vision. We need to pray, 'God open my eyes' and see that there are more for us than against us."

Chapter 3

Life Through A Lens

I remember taking our daughter Hope with me to the doctors one day. As we sat there she was fascinated by an eye test chart that was mounted on the waiting room wall. She began to pass the time and entertain the captive audience gathered in the surgery waiting room by testing her eyesight and that of any other willing volunteers.

Hope found a sense of victory in effortlessly reading the bottom line where the smallest letters were, while I was unable to get past the first few lines. I knew my eyesight wasn't great, but that day I realised how much it had deteriorated without me even noticing. This prompted me to pay a visit to my optician; I was fed up of waving at complete strangers I thought I knew and putting shower gel on my hair instead of shampoo because I couldn't read the label. I decided to see if I could improve my vision and after several consultations I had laser treatment on my eyes to fix my poor sight. The difference was amazing and as I realised how blurred my vision had been, I wondered why I hadn't tackled it sooner. It was my daughter's challenge to read the eye test chart that had provoked me to take action.

Just as a vision chart placed a demand on my physical eyesight, our 'Now What?' moments place demands on our spiritual eyesight. The problems that we face test how well we can see and read a situation. If we have allowed our spiritual vision to deteriorate, we can miss or be blind to seeing the answers that God has for us. In 'Now What?' moments we can often feel that our choices are limited. But what if there are many more possibilities in front of us, we just can't see them? Isn't it worth getting a spiritual eye test to see if you need your vision adjusting? We can often settle for spiritual eyesight that is either long or shortsighted when we need to be asking God for 20/20 vision.

The Magnifying Lens

Some people have a problem with their vision because they are shortsighted. All they can see is what is right in front of them, but look any further and everything is a bit of a blur. In 'Now What?' moments being spiritually shortsighted can cause you to panic because you can only see the problem up close, as if you are looking at it through a magnifying glass. It can end up looking much bigger than it is and make you feel overwhelmed. Your detailed analysis of how bad the situation is prevents you looking past it to a God who is far greater than any circumstance you can ever face in life. Some of the spies who were sent on an important reconnaissance mission to the Promised Land had this problem. The place was flowing with milk and honey just as God had promised but all they could see were the giants that lived there. Their magnifying glass mentality caused them to write themselves off as mere grasshoppers in comparison and exaggerate the size of the challenge. They completely lost sight of what God had said about their future because of their shortsightedness. (Numbers 13:26-28)

However, Joshua and Caleb had a different perspective. Their eyes were set on God and their spiritual vision was sharp. They could see past the giants to the potential of the land. They saw the lush landscape that could become the dwelling place they desired for their families and allowed the promises of God to focus their eyesight. They were looking at the same situation but had a completely different perspective to the other spies. (Numbers 13:30)

The bad report the spies took back to the Israelites had massive implications for the next generation. They should have grown up in the Promised Land, but instead they were forced to live in the harsh, barren desert. We need to be very aware that when we take important decisions without correcting our vision, it doesn't just affect us. In our 'Now What?' moments we mustn't be so shortsighted that we lose perspective. Otherwise we will close doors that God wanted to remain open and we will see no reason to go to the places he wants to send us.

The Telescopic Lens

Telescopes are great for helping you see what is in the distance. They let you focus in on objects that are miles away on the horizon and see what lies ahead in incredible detail. People with telescopic vision are longsighted. They can clearly see the future up ahead but can miss what is right under their nose. We all need to have a clear vision for the future, but we also need to be able to see and deal with what is happening in our lives right now.

The people of Nazareth were longsighted. They were anticipating the arrival of a great deliverer but couldn't see that he was right in front of them. To them Jesus was just Joseph's boy, he seemed far too normal to be anyone special. After all, he came from Nazareth and was born in a dirty stable. This wasn't the grand entrance they were expecting their Saviour to make and their longsightedness meant they overlooked him and didn't realise that God's answer was already with them. Longsightedness can cause people to become overfamiliar with what is around them. They often live believing something better is on the horizon and end up ignoring the miracle that is already happening in their world.

20/20 Vision

When we have clear spiritual vision it changes the way we see our circumstances. It enables us to see beyond the immediate problem to perceive that God is at work behind the scenes. It focuses our mind on the truth that a miracle working God is on our side. The story of Elisha is an amazing example of what life with 20/20 spiritual vision can be like. Elisha's sight was so clear that he had the ability to see what others couldn't. This had already got him into trouble with the King of Aram, because his amazing spiritual eyesight meant that he could even see what ambushes the Arameans were plotting. He kept tipping the King of Israel off and this had enraged the King of Aram so much that he was determined to kill Elisha. (2 Kings 6:8-23)

The king of Aram tried to ambush Elisha who was with his servant. 'Early in the morning a servant of the Holy Man got up and went out. Surprise! Horses and chariots surrounding the city! The young man exclaimed, "Oh, master! What shall we do?"' (2 Kings 6.15 MSG)

This was definitely a 'Now What?' moment for that servant. He went to bed in his tent and woke up in the morning to discover he was surrounded by a vast army. He was caught completely off guard as his panicked reaction shows. Our 'Now What?' moments can often find us in the same position. We are left shocked and surprised when the situation turns bad, the friend hurts us, the illness comes or the job is lost. We can be bewildered by the things we hadn't seen coming in our peripheral vision.

But Elisha was seeing the situation differently; he didn't panic or get stressed, he just said, "'Don't worry about it - there are more on our side than on their side." Then Elisha prayed, "O God, open his eyes and let him see." The eyes of the young man were opened and he saw. A wonder! The whole mountainside full of horses and chariots of fire surrounding Elisha!' (2 Kings 6:16-17 MSG)

Elisha realised that his servant had a problem with his spiritual sight. He could only see who was against them, but Elisha could see the help that was for them. So Elisha prayed for his servant's eyes to be opened so that he could see God's intervention and move from panic to peace.

In 'Now What?' moments we need to pray the same for our lives. 'Oh God, open my eyes. Let me see the situation as you see it. What am I missing, what am I not seeing? God, help me to see this problem as you see it. Help me to get your perspective on this family challenge, or on my child who is away from you.' The first thing we should do in our 'Now What?' moments is to ask God to open our eyes.

A God Perspective

When our eyes are opened we get a God perspective, we see through eyes of faith instead of fear and it changes the way we respond. This shift in perspective creates an atmosphere that helps us to think outside the box and suggest some crazy solutions to seemingly impossible problems. Elisha and his servant were still surrounded by an army that was about to attack, but the plan he came up with to defuse the situation was highly creative.

If he hadn't been able to see the chariots of fire his best plan might have been to run for his life, or to ask God to kill the army, but instead he prayed, 'God, strike them blind.' (2 Kings 6:18 MSG)

I love the fact that Elisha didn't just ask God to kill them, he made a suggestion. When is the last time you suggested something to God? The sharper our spiritual vision is, the more creative we will become in the solutions we ask God for. Elisha's eyesight didn't see the problem; he saw God's protection and his perspective brought peace rather than panic. He began to think up some alternative solutions, like blinding the Aramean army. God wants to work with us and when we suggest answers to our problems, we can be a part of the miracle he provides. Just like the centurion who said to Jesus, 'say the word, and my servant will be healed.' Jesus was amazed that the man didn't ask him to go and touch his servant like most requests he received. The centurion's perspective allowed him to see an answer that didn't even require Jesus being there. If a word can heal then what else can we suggest as a solution? (Matthew 8:8)

God granted Elisha's request and blinded the army that day.

The miracle continued as Elisha called, "This is not the road and this is not the city. Follow me, and I will lead you to the man you are looking for." (2 Kings 6:19) Elisha was having fun with this miracle as he took control of the whole army. Instead of killing Elisha as they had been commanded, they were now blindly following him into Samaria.

Once again, Elisha's vision played an incredible part in what happens next, 'As they entered the city, Elisha prayed, "O God, open their eyes so they can see where they are." God opened their eyes. They looked around - they were trapped in Samaria! When the king of Israel saw them, he said to Elisha, "Father, shall I massacre the lot?"
"Not on your life!" said Elisha. "You didn't lift a hand to capture them, and now you're going to kill them? No sir, make a feast for them and send them back to their master." So he prepared a huge feast for them. After they ate and drank their fill he dismissed them. Then they returned home to their master. The raiding bands of Aram didn't bother Israel anymore.' (2 Kings 6:20-23 MSG)

Elisha's spiritual eyesight was so sharp that he had the ability to resolve the immediate problem and have a long distance perspective that secured Israel's future protection. This kind of 20/20 eyesight can turn our 'Now What?' moments of personal panic into an answer for others.

Alternative Answers

Do you have a standard response in times of crisis? Do you panic like the servant, or want to wipe out the enemy rather than look for an alternative option? If your reaction in a moment of crisis is predictable, then maybe it's time to ask God to open your eyes.

I remember a 'Now What?' moment when Steve and I needed God to bring an answer to our world. We were about to move house, everything was packed into boxes and we were due to get the keys to our new place in just six days. I was just about to leave to go to church for our Cherish ladies conference, when Steve rushed past me with an envelope saying he needed to post it. After being married for so many years, you can just sense when something isn't quite right, so I asked him what it was for. The UK economy was fairly shaky at the time and it turned out that the bank had withdrawn some of our mortgage offer. If we didn't find the money to bridge the gap we would lose our new house. Steve was carrying the weight of this for our family, he panicked and grabbed the obvious answer of taking out a loan. As you can imagine, the interest was fairly extortionate. As we sat and talked it through, I just didn't have a peace about it, so we sat together, tore up the application and thought 'Now What?' We prayed 'God, we need an answer that right now we can't see and we have 24 hours to find it. We are giving this to you.' And I got into my car and drove to church.

I had only been on the road for 20 minutes when Steve called me on my mobile sounding very excited. 'You are never going to believe this,' he said. Someone we knew had called him and said, 'you have been on my heart, do you need an interest free loan by any chance?' This person who hadn't even been on our radar loaned us the exact amount we needed for our mortgage. It was an incredible demonstration of God's provision for our lives.

The fact is, in a 'Now What?' moment, our first response can be to panic and grab the only answer we can see. But sometimes we can end up settling for the equivalent of a high interest loan when God has a debt free one for us. In every situation we face we need to pray, 'God, open my eyes'. We shouldn't always grab the obvious answer because God may have a better solution.

Life Through a Lens

After a family holiday to Disney World, I was excited to watch back the video footage of the trip. But as it played I could see that there was a problem with the camera lens. Condensation had got onto it and all the images were distorted. We had to send the camera for repair to fix its ability to focus and capture images clearly. In a similar way, we have to check our own spiritual lens for distortion and to keep it clear of anything that could end up blurring our vision. I want to suggest a few different lenses that we can look through during our 'Now

What?' moments to enhance our focus and prevent us from taking a distorted picture of the situations we face.

The Devotional Lens

Your devotional lens is like a zoom lens that you can use to get a close up on God. When you use your devotional lens to zoom in to God, it helps you see things that you couldn't see before. It zooms up on God to find his answer to the situation, it helps you see past the crisis and chaos to focus on him alone. Putting a devotional lens on your life will help you to perceive some things that other lenses won't show you, just like Elisha saw the chariots of fire surrounding him. It will steady you and bring peace in the storm so that like Jesus, you can sleep in the boat when everyone else is freaking out. This is a lens we need to spend time using and learning to look through in our every day lives.

The apostle Paul understood the importance of the devotional lens. He was someone who had a severe sight problem until his Damascus road moment when scales literally fell from his eyes and his perspective was changed forever.

When Paul and Silas were locked up in prison and in chains, with no idea what would happen to them, they began to pray and praise God. They focussed their lens on His greatness instead of their circumstances. When you look through your devotional lens, it makes you more aware of the one who can break every link of the chains you are in. It changes your perspective from panic to praise. In 'Now What?' moments we have to use this lens first. We need to capture His presence by turning our devotion to Him instead of focusing on the demands and drama of our challenge. Devotional lens people pray before they speak, sing before they shout and find His voice before they use their own. After Paul and Silas looked through their devotional lens, an answer arrived in an unexpected way. The whole prison shook and their chains fell off. Your devotional lens will liberate you internally, leaving God to liberate you externally. It will help to break the chains from your perspective so that you can see God's promise in the prison.

Maybe you need to spend some time learning to refocus your devotional lens, to pray, shut out the chaos and draw closer to Jesus. Your devotional lens will bring clarity to your confusion and stop fear blurring your view. It will enable you to capture a clearer picture of the situation you are facing.

The Directional Lens

Our directional lens helps us choose what to focus on next. You may be looking across a vast landscape, but a good photographer has the ability to pick out and zoom in on the right part of the picture. It's like scanning the face of a crowd, and then zooming in to capture the priceless expression on your child's face. In 'Now What?' moments there can be many different things demanding our attention and focus. We need to let God be the source of our direction and let him direct our zoom lens.

Jesus was an expert at using His zoom lens. No matter how busy He was or how many crowds He was surrounded by, He had the ability to zoom in on the right person at the right time. In John 4 we read the story of how Jesus zoomed in on a woman who was drawing water from a well. His disciples didn't see the point in stopping to speak to her but Jesus saw what they failed to see. He zoomed in past their prejudice and misconceptions, taking time to focus in on this woman's journey. He focused in on every detail of her life from her history of broken relationships and her longing for real love, to her search for a life giving relationship with her Father God. She hadn't been able to see her own life with clarity until Jesus refocused her perspective. This woman found her Saviour and became a powerful testimony of what Jesus can do in people's lives.

I have had many directional zoom moments in my journey. They have enabled me to see past the crowd; to focus in on the people and places that God wanted to connect me to. This happened one time when I was in the USA speaking at a conference. During the worship at a church service I felt God say, 'turn around. The girl in the orange sweater and jeans at the back of auditorium is to do with your future.' I was in a crowd worshipping when I felt God specifically zoom my heart and attention in on this stranger. She was stood by the doors at the back of the church hall, so I assumed she was an usher.

That stranger was to become one of my dearest friends, Natalie Grant. I didn't know she had an amazing music ministry and she hadn't heard me speak before. We were simply thrown together by God's zoom. As our friendship developed so did the directional lens we viewed our relationship through. We committed to keep looking at why he had joined our hearts and as a result, our friendship moved from being social to spiritual. We began to realise that God had put us together to start a ministry and we zoomed in on his plans. Responding to God's directional zoom has meant that I now work in two nations and we have both made room in our lives for things we hadn't envisaged before. Together we have embarked on new God adventures. We have been able to reach people and travel to places we hadn't even seen on the horizon of our future. This is how God's directional lens works; it will focus your heart on important things that otherwise you could miss.

Let God steer your directional lens so that you can zoom in on what he has for you. Don't miss those God connections, don't be too busy to zoom in and respond. The directional lens can create pivotal connections that can change your 'Now What?' moments forever.

The Destiny Lens

The destiny lens is the big picture lens for your life. It helps you to take in the full panoramic view of what God is doing. Without it you may lock your vision on to the issues you face and become self-absorbed when God needs you to see the big picture. Your life isn't just about you: it's also meant to be about serving others.

Queen Esther learnt to look through the destiny lens. As a young, orphaned teenager she found herself positioned in the palace for "such a time as this." (Esther 4:14). The lens of her life had to come off her own comforts and be refocused onto the potential genocide of the Jewish people. She could have concentrated on her own inadequacies and needs but when God shows you the wide-angle view of a situation, you can't ignore the plight of those around you. The destiny lens moves you from seeing your 'Now What?' moments to noticing the 'Now What?' situations of others. When Esther said 'If I perish, I perish' she didn't just speak up for herself but for an entire generation. (Esther 4:16) This was destiny lens language because she could see that her elevation to such a privileged position was not about her. She knew that it was about many others who were on God's heart. Like Esther, we must also allow this lens to give us a wider view of the world God has placed us in. We must leave the palace and stand with the people; we must speak from destiny, not from self-centred desires. When we learn to use the destiny lens it gives us a fresh perspective on why God has positioned us for such a time as this.

In our 'Now What?' moments we need to become skilled at using the different lenses to look at our lives. We need to capture a clear image of our situation to show us the purpose behind the trial. Our devotional lens will allow His presence to help us see past the problem. Looking through our directional lens will enable us to zoom in on those destiny-defining connections God has for our lives. Looking through the wide-angle lens will give us a bigger perspective and help us to look past our own brokenness, to the brokenness of the world around us. It will cause us to seek an answer that won't just solve our problem; it will provide a solution to the generations we are called to serve.

Perceive It

There have been many times when I have needed my spiritual eyesight correcting. The circumstances didn't change, but how I saw them did. The problem was still there but now I had an answer that I was unable to perceive before. When I first found my Saviour, my vision was changed forever. Before then, I was literally blind to the things of God and to heaven's alternative perspective. But as I walk with Him I have to make sure I'm still seeing things clearly.

So when is the last time you gave yourself a spiritual eye test? Are you seeing correctly through the lens you are viewing your life through, or is it time for you to ask God to update your prescription? A good way to check your spiritual sight is to start asking questions. Am I seeing this situation as God sees it? Do I need to get someone to help me see what I face differently? Do I need to see this person through a lens of grace?

Perhaps you have been looking at the same situation in the same way for far too long and it's time to get God's perspective and try a different approach. It starts by praying, 'God, open my eyes'. Maybe you will begin to see that you are not outnumbered by the enemy, you are surrounded by God. I am committed to getting better at adjusting the lens of my life, to allow answers to come from any direction God chooses. If God can feed a man meat through the beak of a meat eating bird, if he can supply a coin in a fish's mouth, rain down manna from heaven and speak a word through a donkey, I think he has more than one way to answer what you are believing for. So maybe your answer isn't lost, maybe it's not forgotten. Maybe it's already here and all you have to do is perceive it.

Now What?

Tips For Seeing Your Life Through A Lens

1. Give yourself a spiritual eye test to check if you are seeing God's perspective.

2. Don't settle for being long or shortsighted – ask God for his 20/20 vision.

3. Sharpen your spiritual sight - it will help you to see creative, alternative solutions.

4. Learn to use your devotional, directional and destiny lenses - they will help you to see beyond your problems to God's purposes.

5. Seek wide-angled answers that don't just solve your 'Now What?' but bring a solution to others.

"The long way round may cause you to put some things in a coffin that should have instead been given a cushion to rest its head. For God does not see it as dead but merely asleep."

Chapter 4

The Long Way Round

I had never been so desperate to get home. All I wanted to do was be back with our church family and friends and be sleeping in my own bed. I was stranded in the USA and had been living out of a suitcase for seven weeks. I just wanted to get the next flight back to the UK, but it was proving to be a challenge.

As a family we had travelled to America for a few weeks of ministry and vacation and were ready to return home after having a great time away. We were in a hotel in Chicago about to leave when the phone rang with the news that our travel plans would be changing. Thousands of miles away in Iceland, a little volcano had erupted causing big problems. As the volcano spewed out its black ash into the skies of northern Europe, travel chaos erupted and flights everywhere were cancelled due to safety fears. Unfortunately, ours was one of them.

Now What?

After hours of phone calls and desperate attempts to find planes, trains or automobiles to get us home sooner we were told that we wouldn't be able to fly back to the UK for another 12 days. While the kids were overjoyed at the news that they would get extra time off school, I was not so happy. The date we were given for our flight home was the same date I was due to fly back to the USA for a speaking engagement so there was no point returning home. I had to stay for an extra three weeks and after many delays and rescheduled flights, I finally boarded the plane, overjoyed to be heading home.

I remember sitting down and fastening my seatbelt, grinning from ear to ear at the thought of seeing my family and getting back to normality. Then the pilot made an announcement that changed my cheery disposition by saying, 'Ladies and Gentlemen, I am sorry to inform you that we have just received the news that there has been another eruption of the Icelandic volcano, causing further travel chaos in Europe.' I breathed in deeply about to have a minor meltdown when he added, 'you will however be pleased to hear that I will get you back to the UK today, but to avoid the ash cloud we will have to go the long way round.'

I went from a moment of panic at the mention of the word volcano, to a feeling of slight relief at the words 'we will get you there'. I reasoned that even if we were going to take a longer route, at least I would still reach my destination. So

I began to rationalise my reactions and settle in for the long journey. When I resolved to do this, I felt God start using the circumstances of my extended flight to speak to my heart.

In this chapter, I want to explore the challenge of how we navigate those moments when it seems that God's answer is delayed and your dreams are being denied.

The Captain's Voice

So often on our journey we can find ourselves frustrated with God's timing and become weary with waiting for a delayed answer to our urgent prayers. It's in these seasons that we must attune our ear to the voice of Christ, the captain of our lives so that we don't panic and try to press the ejector seat to avoid the delay. It's best to buckle up and make the most of the journey.

In 'Now What?' moments there can be many different people that will speak into your world, some helpful and some that will hijack you. We need to learn how to discern the contribution of each voice and decide what permission, if any, that voice should be given in this process. You should never allow anyone else to replace the captain's voice, because he is the one who is in control of your journey. I have had to learn to listen for the captain's voice above all others. I can't allow my agenda, emotions, family, friends or busyness to drown it out.

The captain's voice on my flight that day was calm and softly spoken. He wasn't upset or concerned about our new route, it was planned and thought through. They had taken on extra meals, fuel and staff to ensure the journey was as comfortable as possible. This re-route was ultimately necessary, placing our safety over our convenience and the same is true on our spiritual journey. God's voice on your long way round will remain calm and steadfast amidst the upheaval of your delay. That is why we must stay tuned in, even if we hit turbulence. (Proverbs 16:9) says, 'In his heart a man plans his course, but the Lord determines his steps.' We need to be willing to let God re-route our lives if necessary and trust him to guide us. During a delay, God is often making a similar announcement to the one that the captain of my flight made, saying, 'Ladies and Gentlemen, I need to let you know I will get you to your prayed for destination, but this time we are going to take the long way round.'

Suddenly Versus Slowly

If we are honest, we all have moments when we hear a story of how God gave someone a life-changing breakthrough and think, 'Lord, it isn't fair!' They share how they miraculously had a debt paid or were healed, sometimes without seeming to have even asked God for it. We end up feeling that God may have lost interest in our battle and question His love for us. When left unanswered, these kinds of questions can make us give up on ever getting our own victory and decide it's too hard to fight for our miracle anymore.

This is why we need to not only know and applaud the God of the instant miracle testimonies but also learn to love and appreciate the same God that takes us the long way round. We need to make room for more testimonies of those that held fast for the answers that didn't come as quickly. We need to applaud more often the process that people went through and the lessons they learned through their long way round. We need a mature revelation of God that captures his power in both journeys. When I heard God whisper to my heart about the long way round on my flight home, I began to see how the Bible is full of answers that came suddenly and also those that came slowly. The good news is that just like my extended flight home, both get you to your intended destination and both demonstrate the awesome love and power of God.

Smashing Jars or Battle Scars

Just think for a moment about warriors like Gideon and Joshua. They were both young men who were chosen by God. Both had to take on the challenge of leading God's people into battle and both of them needed breakthroughs. Yet when Gideon faced the Midianites, God gave them straight into his hands. He instructed Gideon and his army to smash a few jars and blow into their trumpets to win the battle. They didn't even have to raise their swords as God terrified the enemy causing them to panic and run away. All Gideon's men had to do was go and collect as much plunder as they could carry and then return home in time for supper. Gideon had an instant victory that night!

The victory wasn't quite so easy for Joshua. He had to fight one of the longest, most exhausting battles recorded. Joshua had to fight for so long that he prayed in a way that didn't even make sense. He asked for the sun to stand still because the light was fading but the battle was still raging. The victory that night was going to be one he fought long and hard for and one that would cost many lives. But I love how Joshua didn't pray that God would stop the battle, he just asked for more sunlight. In his long battle he refused to quit but kept going, believing and obeying God. He knew that God could wipe out any army He chose to. Perhaps that would have been a simpler miracle than asking for the world to stop turning to delay the sunset. Joshua understood that the long way round didn't change the fact that God was on his side, it just changed how God intervened in this situation. He knew that victory would come and he was willing to trust God whether it came suddenly or slowly. What an inspiration he is to our lives when we face battles. We all want to smash jars but Joshua was willing to get battle scars.

Shout or Crawl

It was the same for those who Jesus healed. Some people in the crowd simply shouted his name and at the sound of their pain and distress Jesus stopped. He silenced the masses to minister to them and with one touch or a word they were healed. People like the blind man who shouted to Jesus and had his sight restored, or the crippled man who was sat begging. Jesus gave them a gift worth far more than money by healing them. That day the men walked away from their infirmity to a life of freedom.

Yet it doesn't always happen like this. One woman had to crawl and push past her embarrassment and exhaustion to receive her miracle. She had suffered from severe bleeding for 12 long years and had visited many doctors, but no one could help her. She dragged her aching body through a crowd and crawled through people's feet to touch the hem of Jesus' garment. Despite her utter desperation she kept believing that she could and would get her miracle, even if it happened on a very long way round.

One of the most striking examples of suddenly and slowly answers can be seen in the lives of two very different families. Both needed a miracle of Gods' resurrection power for loved ones who had died. One family received an instant answer while the others had to wait much longer, so let's consider some lessons from their long way round.

The Suddenly

Luke 7 describes how a widow was conducting the funeral of her only child when Jesus passed by. There is no record to suggest this woman was a believer or had prayed for a miracle. It appears that she had accepted that her son was gone and was mourning her loss.

But that day, Jesus decided to provide a 'suddenly' answer. 'As they approached the village gate, they met a funeral procession - a woman's only son was being carried out for burial. And the mother was a widow. When Jesus saw her, his heart broke. He said to her, "Don't cry." Then He went over and touched the coffin. The pallbearers stopped. He said, "Young man, I tell you: Get up." The dead son sat up and began talking. Jesus presented him to his mother.'
(Luke 7:11-15 MSG)

Jesus was just passing by that day. He was on His way to another destination when this family caught His attention and He felt their pain and grief. His heart was moved so He stretched out His hand, touched the coffin and the boy was resurrected. Can you imagine the scene that must have unfolded when the dead boy suddenly came back to life? Tears of mourning became tears of joy and hope returned to this widow. She swapped a heartbreaking loss for a joyous reunion. The excitement of her friends and relatives must have been immense with screams of awe resonating around the town. This was a 'wow' moment when Jesus demonstrated His love, compassion and power in an instant.

We all love these stories and we teach them to ignite faith in the hearts of those who have lost hope for their miracle. This kind of quick intervention is what we pray for in our own times of desperation. Or we seek out gatherings where these breakthroughs are promised, hoping that God will meet us there. Although God can bring the miraculous to our world, we must be mindful that He will answer us in His way, not ours.

With our natural children we love to step in and help when they need us. But there are times when we must resist instantly intervening because they have lessons to learn and growth to gain through their struggle. God is our Heavenly Father and we also have to allow for His chosen method of parenting His children. He may provide an instant answer for one, but decide to take another the long way round because He sees that the journey will ultimately benefit them.

So, let's examine the story of another family who needed a resurrection miracle. This family were close friends of Jesus. Often the longer we serve and love Christ, the more we can begin to assume that we should be first in the queue when it comes to answered prayers. If we are aware of God acting suddenly, then it can become harder to be kept waiting as we see others receive their answer quickly. However, this is exactly what the family of Lazarus had to navigate as God took them the long way round.

Is Jesus Late?

John 11 tells the story of 'A man was sick, Lazarus of Bethany, the town of Mary and her sister Martha. This was the same Mary who massaged the Lord's feet with aromatic oils and then wiped them with her hair. It was her brother, Lazarus, who was sick. So the sisters sent word to Jesus, "Master, the one you love so very much is sick."
When Jesus got the message, he said, "This sickness is not fatal. It will however become an occasion to show God's glory by glorifying God's Son." He stayed on where he was for two more days. (John 11:4)

I love how this family sent out their urgent request to Jesus. The detail they included in it by saying, 'the one you love so very much is sick' shows how close they felt their relationship with Him was. The sisters' words imply that they were His faithful friends; they are letting Jesus know that they think they are different from the crowd. They believed their friendship with Jesus was enough to get them a quick response. It's amazing how when we hit a crisis we can often pray in a similar way. 'Don't you remember me God? I'm the one you love so you need to answer me immediately!'

Jesus didn't ignore their request. His reply was 'this isn't fatal.' Yet, in 'Now What?' moments those words can often get lost in translation. If we miss hearing God's announcement then we can end up jeopardising the whole journey. The news that Lazarus' sickness was not going to be fatal should have become the fuel for their faith on the long way round. Jesus perspective on the situation was very different. The delay wasn't due to a lack of concern, it was because Lazarus' 'Now What?' moment had a wider purpose that Jesus was about to unfold.

Heavenly Perspective

In 'Now What?' moments we need to understand that heaven's perspective of our situation is often very different to ours. All that Mary and Martha could see was that Jesus needed to change his plans and come straight away. But Jesus didn't see an illness that was fatal, so he took their demand and added divine delay. It was this delay that allowed enough time for Lazarus' condition to worsen and for the problem to be upgraded from sickness requiring a healing, to death needing a resurrection.

God's perspective on our 'Now What?' moments is surprising at times. Jesus told his disciples that Lazarus had simply fallen asleep and that He was going to wake him up. The disciples didn't understand what He meant by that, and I am sure that Mary and Martha in the midst of their grief didn't see it that way either.

The story continues, 'The disciples said, "Master, if he's gone to sleep, he'll get a good rest and wake up feeling fine." Jesus was talking about death, while his disciples thought he was talking about taking a nap. Then Jesus became explicit: "Lazarus died. And I am glad for your sakes that I wasn't there. You're about to be given new grounds for believing. Now let's go to him."' (John 11:12-14 MSG)

In our 'Now What?' moments we need to understand that God's timing is not the same as ours and our idea of urgent is not his. Our panic finds Him in peace and what causes us stress doesn't even register with Him. When a situation worsens because God's answer is delayed we need to seek a perspective shift. Lazarus was dead as far as his family and the disciples were concerned, but to Jesus, he was simply taking a nap!

Dead or Asleep?

Perhaps on our long way round journeys we end up mourning over things in our lives that we think are dead when God sees them as only asleep. If you were to change the way you see your situation, would you be acting differently right now? If you could see your dream asleep and not dead, what would you try to achieve in life? Or, if you could see your marriage as being asleep but not dead, how differently would you speak about it and hold on to it? The long way round delay may cause you to put something in a coffin that should only have been given a cushion to rest its head on. That's why we must listen for God's voice in 'Now What?' moments. We need to allow for delays and not be so quick to plan a burial if we should be planning for an occasion instead.

I had a major 'Now What?' moment several years ago when Steve and I were told by a doctor that I wouldn't be able to conceive. As I sat facing the clinical diagnosis my heart cried out 'Now What?' 'Where is God in this?' 'How can this be right?' After recovering from the shock we quickly got our prayer requests into God, with a note asking to make it happen as soon as possible. We expected a sudden miracle, a quick intervention like the widow in Luke 7 received. I didn't want or understand the Jesus who added extra time to his trip when Lazarus needed him the most.

To be honest, when I was faced with endless hospital visits to try and help me have a baby, I started to become annoyed with other women I knew who seemed to get pregnant with ease. I felt God challenge me in that time of disappointment to change my behaviour to, 'Sing O barren woman, you who never bore a child; burst into song.' (Isaiah 54:1) That is not the behaviour you would expect from someone when their dream appears to be dead, but it's the behaviour you may need if you ever want to receive your miracle.

For me, this change from mourning to singing made me realise that I could either spend time worrying and harbouring disappointment or choose to water the seeds for my future. So, I started throwing baby showers for as many pregnant girls in our church as I could find. This helped me to gain a heavenly perspective, that maybe my womb wasn't dead but simply asleep.

It's Not About You

Personally, I found that this experience strengthened my faith and resilience, but there was far more to it. My journey wasn't just about me, it was also about the people I would meet on the way. When you take the long way round it brings others across your path that you would never have met if God had taken you on a more direct route. Your journey can be part of their answer and part of their miracle too.

I remember a couple visiting the church as we were going through a difficult time when each cycle of fertility treatment had failed. They weren't Christians and came forward for prayer. No one told me their situation, but I heard God whisper to my heart, 'They want a baby. Pray for their miracle.' Everything inside me wanted to walk in the other direction because I didn't want to pray for their miracle when I hadn't received my own. I remember secretly arguing with

God saying, 'they don't even call you Lord! Why would you ask me to pray for them when you haven't answered my prayers?' My attempts to dissuade God failed and He said, 'pray for them.' So I did, although I have to admit I had a bad attitude about it.

Just two months later they came back to church with smiling faces. 'We have some amazing news! I'm pregnant!' she said. I congratulated them but I was battling with my own feelings and a sense of disappointment. I struggled to understand why God would do this for people who weren't even believers, when I was left facing the same situation without an answer. I shared an affinity with how Mary and Martha must have felt when they asked Jesus to come and he chose to stay longer with people he hardly knew instead.

As I recall my journey for this book, I can testify about our two beautiful gifts from God who came into our life. First, our beautiful daughter Hope Cherish, and then a few years later our incredible son, Noah Brave. This is where the beauty of the delay becomes clearer. Noah and Hope were our answer to prayer, but because we had to take the long way round our story has become a beacon of hope to thousands of others facing the same situation. The point is, God has a far greater purpose for taking you the long way round than it just being about you and your need or problem.

Now What?

Jesus took the long way round so that he could pick up more passengers and change more lives than just this family's. It wasn't only about resurrecting Lazarus; it was about resurrecting faith and hope in Mary and Martha. It was about challenging the thinking of His disciples and people's perception of who He was. He didn't just want it to be about Lazarus, He wanted to include many other people in the miracle.

When Jesus finally arrived in Bethany he found two grieving, disappointed sisters and started to unravel the 'Now What?' of disappointment and doubt. In the next chapter we'll find out what happened next when Jesus invited them to take a walk with him.

Now What?

Tips For The Long Way Round

1. Tune in and listen to the captain's voice in your life.

2. Know that He is the God of the suddenly and of the long way round – both get you to your destination.

3. Get a heavenly perspective. Maybe some things in your life are not dead but just asleep.

4. Change your behaviour to match your believing.

5. Remember that it's not just about you – the long way round includes others in your miracle.

"Let your weakness be held

by His strength for in your

vulnerability you will see

His majesty"

Chapter 5

Let's Take A Walk

Have you ever had one of those conversations that starts with 'let's take a walk?' You know instinctively that the person inviting you to join them wants to share some things that you may not want to hear. Their attempt to separate you from the noise, demands and usual daily routine of your life is a clue that they have something important to say that they don't want you to miss. I have found that some of the most difficult walks I have taken with God are in my 'Now What?' moments. They are the times when your plans are not coming together as you had hoped and you feel disorientated about which direction to take. Often in these times, God takes the opportunity to break into our routine with the invitation for us to 'take a walk'.

Jesus was someone who invited others to take a walk with him. In their 'Now What?' moments He would often draw alongside and walk with them for a while. The walks were full of purpose, they were about refocusing their thoughts and often about re-routing their steps. He walked with Peter after his denial, He walked with James and John to settle their ambitious demands, and He walked with some confused and disillusioned disciples on the road to Emmaus. So, let's see what happened on their journey.

Walk This Way

The long walk from Jerusalem to Emmaus was a major 'Now What?' moment for these disciples because they thought that Jesus had left them forever. They had given up hope for His resurrection and were questioning their future career options. All their points of identity and safety seemed to have been removed. Jerusalem had become a place of persecution for them and Jesus' return was outside the time frame that their faith would allow them to wait. So they decided to walk away. I love how the first thing Jesus asked when He joined them was, 'What are you discussing as you walk?' The fact is, when we take a walk without God the discussions we take part in can be unhelpful to our destination. 'Now What?' moments can create such a lack of clarity and confusion that we need to be guarded about what conversations we take part in. These disciples were letting fear shape their discussion and the purpose of their walk was to escape conflict.

It's in these moments that we must allow Jesus to walk alongside us. His influence will change our conversation and simplify the options for what we should do next. Jesus began to remind them of the truth of the word, He questioned their unbelief, asked them many questions about why they doubted. It wasn't until the end of their walk that they realised that this fellow traveller was not a stranger but their Saviour and they said, 'were not our hearts burning within us while He talked with us on the road?'

When God joins your walk the conversation will always leave you with the same feeling. At first you may not like what you hear, because it challenges where you are at. You may want to discuss your disappointment but when God enters the conversation, He starts to refocus you and increase your spiritual temperature and capacity.

(Proverbs 24:10) says, 'If you falter in times of trouble, how small is your strength!' I think the walk helps us to take stock of our spiritual stamina for the journey. It's in those times of testing that we realise what we are lacking.

I have taken many of these walks during my 'Now What?' moments and I have had to confront my own unbelief and face up to my lack of faith. Yet, God has never used these walks to judge me, embarrass me or expose my failings. Many times, he has taken me to a place that was hidden from others. He isolated me for my own protection so that I couldn't hear the negative voices of others who were trying to speak into the dilemmas I faced. As we walked together, I let my weakness be held by His strength and in the vulnerability that these moments created I became very aware of His majesty. In fact, these walks have become some of the most pivotal moments in my journey of knowing God and trusting Him.

Jesus is not afraid of answering difficult questions, so be honest in your conversation. Don't avoid the walk because this is your opportunity to be real with Him, to deal with your doubts and to get back on course with God's plan, just like the disciples did. For them, it meant making a complete u-turn and walking the seven miles back to Jerusalem where they should have been waiting for Him all along.

Back to Bethany

So, let's take a look at another one of these walks by going back to the story of Lazarus. A few days after Lazarus' death, Jesus invited the disciples to take a walk with him back to Bethany. Their response was less than enthusiastic and one of the disciples even said 'Let us also go, that we may die with Him.' (John 11:16)

For the disciples, this was a walk back to a hostile environment because they had left the town of Bethany after facing persecution and opposition. They didn't understand why Jesus would want to go back there, especially as His return would now be to a grieving family because he hadn't answered their call for help in time. For Jesus, the walk had a greater purpose because the disciples would be given new grounds for believing. The distance from Jerusalem to Bethany was only a few miles, but the greatest distance the disciples would travel as they walked with Jesus wasn't geographical. His intention was that they would cover a far greater distance in their thinking and in their faith. Jesus was walking the disciples to a greater level of understanding and a deeper appreciation of who He was.

When Jesus joins you for a walk, often He wants to prepare your heart for what comes next and to galvanise your faith. The walk is all about settling your heart, calming your doubts and getting you ready for the next step. Jesus knew that when the disciples reached Bethany they would be faced with people asking the same questions they themselves had on their walk. The disciples would have to answer people's doubt, unbelief and accusations about Jesus turning up late. Even the disciple who had first said, 'Let's go and die with Him' was now ready to go and stand with Jesus. They were all better prepared to greet a grieving family and a distressed Martha who was about to have her own experience of taking a walk with Jesus.

Control Freak

Martha was one of those 'take charge' personalities. It's as if nothing ever seemed to phase her. She was very cross with her younger sister Mary for sitting at Jesus' feet while she was trying be Masterchef in the kitchen all on her own! I can relate to Martha, she was the older sister and as the eldest of four girls, I understand how she was wired. You take on the responsibility to look after your siblings, to organise everyone and take control and this is just what Martha did when Lazarus died. (Luke 10: 38-41)

For me, Martha is the classic case of a control freak. Her heart is in the right place but her overwhelming urge to have things under control often meant she let her head take over. If your nature is to take control, then taking the long way round is your worst nightmare because it messes with your schedules and plans. Often we don't notice our control freak tendencies until we feel totally out of control. This is what Martha's 'Now What?' moment exposed in her life. She couldn't deal with her sense of disappointment so she went on a damage limitation exercise and tried to manage the situation when Jesus didn't show up in accordance with her plan.

A control freak always has another plan and often they are very resourceful people. If plan 'A' fails, then they have plan 'B', 'C' and 'D' already lined up. Martha quickly took control and moved on after plan 'A' failed when Jesus didn't arrive in time. By the time He did show, up her brother was dead and buried. I am sure that she was the one who had organised the funeral, looked after everyone, made sure the house was spotless and catered for all the visitors and mourners. On the surface she looked like someone who was coping admirably and who had it all together, but Jesus' arrival caused cracks to appear and her controlled exterior came under pressure.

Martha loved Jesus and yet she couldn't understand why on this occasion in her opinion he was too late. She greets Jesus in a way that leaves him in no doubt that she is upset with his seemingly tardy arrival. She said, 'Lord, if you had been here, my brother would not have died.' (John 11:21)

Martha had already tidied up the situation in her own mind and dealt with it. Her brother was dead, it was over and Jesus' late arrival wasn't going to change anything. The only problem was she had also managed Jesus out of the situation too.

The Door of Possibility

Martha's controlling nature meant that she had already tied up the loose ends and had shut the door to believing Lazarus could live. But Jesus saw it differently, He knew that the door was still open and there was space for a new possibility.

Now What?

The conversation that happened next was amazing. Jesus answered Martha's analysis of what had gone wrong with the possibility of what could still happen.

'Jesus said, "Your brother will be raised up."
Martha replied, "I know that he will be raised up in the resurrection at the end of time."
"You don't have to wait for the End. I am, right now, Resurrection and Life. The one who believes in me, even though he or she dies, will live. And everyone who lives believing in me does not ultimately die at all. Do you believe this?" (John 11:23-26 MSG)

Jesus wanted to know how much Martha really believed in Him, but she had let her unbelief and disappointment cause her to downscale her miracle from Lazarus being healed to seeing him one day in heaven. Maybe this was her way of coping and staying strong.

When Jesus says Lazarus can live, her reply sounds more like a statement that she has rehearsed than a declaration of faith that the situation can turn around. She tidied up Jesus' suggestion with a scripture about the end times. It's amazing how in hard times we can even quote scriptures and sound like we are being spiritual, when in reality we are just using them to try to explain away our disappointment and the failure of what we thought was God's plan.

Maybe Martha's faith remained when her brother was still breathing, even if his breath was slow and painful. The cut off point for her faith which caused her 'Now What?' moment was when Lazarus drew his last breath. That was when she moved on from praying and believing to shutting the door firmly behind her. Often our controlling nature can close doors that God wants us to leave open.

If you are a Martha kind of personality you might also try to take control in the midst of your 'Now What?' moments, to the point that when God steps into your situation, you have already organised him out of it. You have chosen to manage without your miracle to minimise your disappointment.

In the middle of your 'Now What?' moments, God will often challenge you about what you really believe. Do you really believe that He is the God of miracles who can do the impossible? Do you really believe that He can intervene on your journey? 'Do you believe that your family can be saved? Do you believe that your marriage can be restored? Do you believe that your sickness can be healed? If you are facing a situation that looks hopeless do you believe that God can still resurrect it?

God doesn't want us to simply quote scripture, anybody can recite lines or memorise a verse. God is looking past the words into your heart to see the real convictions of your faith.

Now What?

The fact is, when a trial comes and the unexpected happens it will expose any gaps between the confession of your mouth and the true conviction of your heart.

Emotional Basket Case

Despite being sisters, Mary and Martha were total opposites when it came to their personality types. Martha was fantastic at staying in control where as Mary was a highly emotional character. Yet just as Jesus wanted to unravel Martha's control, he also wanted to help her over emotional younger sister. From the moment Jesus first enters the village we see such a contrast between the two. Martha went out to meet him on a damage limitation exercise, where as Mary the archetypal emotional basket case didn't even realise he had arrived because she was too busy wailing and weeping in a soggy mess on the floor.

Maybe in your 'Now What?' moments, you are more of a Mary than a Martha. Instead of taking control, you lose it and don't care who sees that you're upset. In fact, you don't hide your disappointment you dramatise it. You are, let's say, emotionally free and highly expressive with your feelings.

In true Mary fashion, when she heard that Jesus was asking for her she ran to him and threw herself at his feet, still weeping.

'She jumped up and ran out to Him.' Jesus had not yet entered the town but was still at the place where Martha had met Him. When her sympathising Jewish friends saw Mary run off, they followed her, thinking she was on her way to the tomb to weep there. Mary came to where Jesus was waiting and fell at his feet, saying, "Master, if only you had been here, my brother would not have died."' (John 11:24-32 MSG)

Mary had already grown her own emotional support group. She had sympathising friends around her to console her and share in her tears. I have found that emotion likes to be with company, it likes to feel it has a crying partner. It ensures that when the drama hits it will have an audience of willing supporters.

Mary was not doing anything wrong in grieving but the grieving had become all she was doing. Lazarus had been dead for days but she was still crying. She had been crying for so long that when she did go to meet Jesus, her personal support group were so used to her emotional drama that they presumed she was simply changing weeping positions.

I want to be clear that being emotional is not wrong, we all need to be able to express our grief, we need to be able to weep, to be angry and show our frustration. I have often sat with people who have cried about their 'Now What?' moment. But sometimes I am the fourth or fifth person they have cried with over the same issue. At some point you have to gently point out to people that their tears are clouding their view and its time for them to change their countenance to reflect Christ's. Jesus didn't judge Mary for her emotion, he empathised and in fact he later wept himself. But Jesus' tears were purposeful and appropriate. I believe we have to be able to find that place of appropriate emotion.

Jesus wasn't impressed by Mary's tears. 'When Jesus saw her sobbing and the Jews with her sobbing, a deep anger welled up within him. He said, "Where did you put him?"
"Master, come and see," they said. 'Now Jesus wept'. (John 11:33-35 MSG)

Mary and Jesus both wept over the loss of Lazarus, someone they loved. Yet Jesus handled his emotions very differently to Mary. He expressed anger and empathy, but in a measured way that fitted the situation. The way He dealt with the situation inspires and encourages me to stay in charge of my emotions. On the long way round when you are faced with difficulty it can be too easy to let your emotions take over. It is very hard to see clearly when your eyes are clouded by tears. Emotions can take you down ditches you don't need to be in and sometimes blur your eyes to the exit ramp that God is providing. They are guaranteed to make you more mindful of your own pain than of the promises God has made you.

Don't Forget the Great Occasion

When Jesus first heard Lazarus was sick, He told the disciples that the sickness would not be fatal, but it would be a great occasion. Here we have one of the reasons God takes us the long way round. An occasion is something that people gather for. It is an event that people remember; they talk about it for a long time afterwards and frame the photo they took as a keep sake to remind them. An occasion involves many more people than just you and this is why God uses them. God doesn't just use the long way round to just reach you but he uses it to pick up as many people on the way as Lazarus' miracle shows.

Jesus arrived in Bethany to find many Jews visiting Martha and Mary, sympathising with them over their brother; a crowd was gathering. He knew what he was doing. A crowd wouldn't have gathered if Lazarus had been sick and then healed, but they came because Lazarus had died and they knew that Jesus was his friend. I imagine some of His critics saw it as a good opportunity to bring Jesus down and critical comments were heard in the crowd. Some said, "If He loved him so much why didn't He do something to keep him from dying? After all, He opened the eyes of a blind man.'" (John 11:37 MSG)

The Critics

Jesus knew that this occasion would gather those who loved Him and those that loathed Him. The fact is, when we have a disappointment in our life we often receive two sets of visitors, those who want us to believe and those who want to prove their unbelief. Many times, I have heard people share how when they felt God had failed them, others from their past offered sympathy saying, 'This God thing isn't what you need, this faith thing is faulty,' or 'If God is so good then why are you sick?' Unbelieving friends who lack faith have seen this as a way to justify their unbelief. As far as many people in Bethany were concerned, Jesus had failed by letting his friend die and the critics were gathering with their comments. In our 'Now What?' moments the critics often gather to voice their opinion and the unexpected email or counsel you receive from someone who previously had nothing to say to you is awkward or discouraging.

Jesus knew the critics would gather and it didn't bother Him. He wanted them to be there because they would also be part of the very great occasion that He had spoken of before Lazarus died. I'm sure He wanted as many people as possible to gather around the tomb that day. From the beginning, He had planned that the long way round would not only involve a demonstration of His resurrection power but it would also put to death the rumours and criticism that came from the people of Bethany.

I love what happened next. 'Then Jesus, the anger again welling up within Him, arrived at the tomb. It was a simple cave in the hillside with a slab of stone laid against it. Jesus said, "Remove the stone." The sister of the dead man, Martha, said, "Master, by this time there's a stench. He's been dead four days!"' (John 11 38-39 MSG)

Notice that at this point that Martha was again trying to take control by trying to stop Jesus from exposing a bad smell. I am sure at this point she was looking for her air freshener and scented candles to at least minimise the embarrassment.

'Jesus looked her in the eye. "Didn't I tell you that if you believed, you would see the glory of God?" Then, to the others, "Go ahead, take away the stone." They removed the stone. Jesus raised his eyes to heaven and prayed, "Father, I'm grateful that you have listened to me. I know you always do listen, but on account of this crowd standing here I've spoken so that they might believe that you sent me." Then he shouted, "Lazarus, come out!" And he came out, a cadaver, wrapped from head to toe, and with a kerchief over his face. Jesus told them, "Unwrap him and let him loose." (John 11:40-44)

Now that's what you call an occasion Jesus style. As Jesus prays He silenced the critics, challenged their beliefs and called forth a dead man who is wrapped from head to toe in bandages. In that moment I am sure that the critics went quiet, tears of grief were turned into shouts of joy and doubting disciples stood and watched in awe. Not only was Lazarus alive once again, but so were the dreams, expectations and understanding of all those gathered. God wants to do the same for those who are included on our long way round journeys.

Many who read the story of Lazarus are drawn to how sensational it was, but the only miracle they see is the moment he was raised from the dead. Bringing Lazarus back to life was actually the easy part. The biggest challenge on this long way round was challenging the unbelief, silencing fear, renewing trust and injecting a faith lift into the lives of those Jesus called friends.

Double for Your Trouble

It's interesting to compare the two resurrection stories recorded in the gospels of the widow who got her instant miracle and Lazarus who took the long way round. I can see that although the widow got her son back, Lazarus' family didn't only get him back, they gained far more. The journey they took built faith and strength into their lives, painful as it may have been at times, they came out of it different. Their journey with Jesus changed them on the inside and touched the lives of many others who became part of it. What the long way round achieves in you and through you, will see you gain double for your trouble. So, in your 'Now What?' delay, if you are questioning why God hasn't shown up yet, keep going and maximise the extra miles that God is adding to your miracle.

Now What?

Tips For Taking A Walk

1. Take the talk walk with God.

2. Deal with your control issues. Calm the emotional hijacker.

3. Face the questions so that you can face them for others.

4. Don't worry if critics gather, invite them to the party.

5. Pick up double for your trouble in the lives around you.

"God wants to grab your attention

and play for you showreels of

hope. They are 'coming soon'

trailers for your future to sustain

you in present trials."

Chapter 6

The God Grab

I don't know about you, but when I go to see a movie, I'm one of those annoying people who have to call the cinema to ask what time the film actually starts. I'm not sure whether it's because I'm impatient or just because I know my kids won't sit still for very long, so I want to avoid an extra twenty minutes of trailers and commercials. I will even endure the endless automated answer phone options that most cinemas have and persevere until I get to speak to a real person who can answer my question. As a mum, I have discovered that avoiding the trailers also saves me from buying even more popcorn and extra toilet breaks. I like to keep the stress to a minimum by arriving just as the movie starts.

However, I once went to see a movie with a friend and didn't get to phone up in advance. We arrived as the trailers started and I reluctantly sat down to watch them as I waited for the main feature to begin. At that moment I felt God nudge my impatient spirit and start to speak to me through my trailer watching experience. I began to see that the trailers had a greater significance than I realised. They were there to give me a glimpse of what was 'coming soon'.

The 'Coming Soon'

My tightly scheduled way of movie watching meant that I was only interested in my pre-selected film choice. But as I sat waiting that day, I began to see all the movies that were coming soon play out on the screen in front of me. As I watched the action-packed trailers I began to get excited about seeing a new film that I hadn't heard of before. I laughed at funny snippets from a script I didn't know had been written and I was drawn into the plot of a story yet to be told.

As I watched, God reminded me that He also had 'coming soon' trailers for my life, yet my impatience often prevented me from seeing them. God's trailers show us the things that are on their way so we need to sit up and pay attention to them. In our 'Now What?' moments, catching a glimpse of what is 'coming soon' can revive our hope when we face hopeless situations. It can strengthen our spirit when we feel worn out and ready to quit.

God's trailers are His way of gripping your heart, to help you see beyond your circumstances and give you the courage to keep going. God has many different trailers that He wants to play for us that are show reels of hope about our cities, our families and the world. We need to become avid viewers of God's trailers, to look up from our 'Now What?' moments and allow our faith to rise as we see what is 'coming soon'.

The God Grab

Ezekiel was known as 'God's watchman' and as a prophet his job was to show people the trailers that God had for their lives. You might think that sounds like a great job, but after a while Ezekiel became despondent because people just weren't interested in the prophecies he was bringing. They didn't want to watch the 'coming soon' trailers that God had for their lives. (Ezekiel 33:30-32)

Ezekiel was seen as a form of entertainment; they would listen to him talk but did nothing about what they heard. It wasn't easy playing God's prophetic trailers to an audience who were indifferent. So God gripped Ezekiel's heart again by playing him a trailer for the House of Israel that he could not ignore.

I love how The Message Bible describes God interrupting Ezekiel's journey. 'God grabbed Ezekiel.' (Ezekiel 37:1) When someone grabs you it jolts you out of your routine. A grab demands your attention and pulls you closer to the one who has a grip on you. Although Ezekiel was still committed to serving God, he was discouraged by the lack of response to his message, so God grabbed him. We can also be following and serving God, but lose the passion that used to be attached to our purpose. Weariness, disappointment and difficulties can overshadow God's grip on our heart. In those moments we need to be grabbed by Him all over again.

Sometimes at home I call across the kitchen to my son Noah as he sits focused on his computer game. I can call his name, once, twice or even three times but he is so engrossed in what he is doing that he doesn't hear me or respond to my voice. He is too busy playing his game; slaying a dragon, digging for treasure, or solving a puzzle. He is in the same room but totally unaware of what is happening around him. Eventually, I have to go across the room, take his face in my hands and say his name again. At this point he wonders why I am so frustrated and keen to have his attention and I have to explain that he hadn't heard me call his name.

When I read how God grabbed Ezekiel, I imagine it could have been similar to the way I cross the room to talk to Noah. Sometimes your Heavenly Father doesn't just want to call your name but to hold your face in his hands so that he has your full attention. This is what happened to Ezekiel and his moment with God renewed his affection for the people he was sent to reach.

Grabbed For Purpose

God can grab us for many different reasons. His grab can focus us back on his purpose for our lives. His grab can prevent us from going in the wrong direction and ending up off course. His grab can reconnect us with Him and be used to connect us to others who have an important role to play in what's 'coming soon' for our lives.

When I look back over my life I can see that when I allowed God to grab my attention, His grab led me to a pivotal connection for my future. There was a purpose for it and the grab propelled me forward in my 'Now What?' moment. I remember one time God grabbed my heart and challenged me to start a ministry to honour women. It was the night before our women's conference and I was focusing intently on my final preparations. I was under pressure and weighed down with so much work for the event and in the middle of being preoccupied with many other things, God called my name and grabbed my heart. As I gave God my full attention, he played me a trailer of hope that featured the lives of courageous women. I knew he wanted me to play a part in making it happen and because I allowed God to grab my heart that day, the Cherish Foundation was born. The foundation honours women who have faced heartbreaking 'Now What?' moments and celebrates how they have triumphed over adversity.

God crossed the room that day to lift my head and grab my heart for these women. I didn't feel under pressure but felt an incredible passion to start this ministry that has brought hope to so many women. To this day, the foundation is one of the most special things I get to be involved with. It's as if when God grabs you, He can anoint you to do things you didn't even know were possible. We must pay attention to God grabs because they are always about a bigger purpose.

God grabbed my heart on another occasion when I first heard an amazing woman called Marilyn Skinner speak. One moment I was listening to her incredible story and the next I was gripped by God. I felt compelled to connect with her and find out how I could play a part in supporting Watoto, the ministry she and her husband set up to rescue orphaned children and former child soldiers in Uganda. As God arrested my heart that day, I had no idea that it would lead to a purposeful partnership, building a school in Uganda and rescuing more lives. Responding to that God grab has changed my life and our church forever. Only heaven can tell how many lives will be rescued because of it.

God Lifts and Sets

But God didn't just grab Ezekiel, that was only the beginning and it's important we continue to read on. After the grab, came the lift. It says in Ezekiel, 'God grabbed me and then God's spirit took me up and he set me down.' God first grabs you to get your attention, then he lifts you, and finally he sets you back down. (Ezekiel 37:1-2 MSG)

In our 'Now What?' moments we need to understand the importance of letting God lift us. God lifts give you a new perspective of the situation you are in and can raise the level of your faith. Ezekiel's vision and confession needed lifting when he faced a people who had hardened their hearts towards God. We need the same kind of lift when we are facing our 'Now What?' moments.

Often we pray that God would lift us out of the circumstances we are in. But when God grabs you and lifts you up, He always sets you back down in the circumstance He has called you to help change. He doesn't lift you up so that you can escape your 'Now What?' moments or become immune from your problems. He simply wants you to gain a different view and see what He knows is 'coming soon'. The lift will enable you to declare his goodness in hard times and see past the problem to His promises. We need to be people who co-operate with the God lift and be willing to let Him challenge our mindset and lift our thinking. It starts with us building a life that is easy for God to lift.

A Life That Lifts

I don't know if you have ever tried to lift a child who doesn't want to move, but it can be very difficult. When you announce that it's bedtime they say no and somehow adopt an immovable position. Usually it would be easy to pick them up and they would reach out their arms towards you to be lifted. But when they don't want to move they become like a dead weight on your sofa. Their body posture goes into sink mode. Their legs are locked into position, their muscles are tense and their arms refuse to reach out to you.

We can do exactly the same spiritually. God wants to grab us, but we fold our arms, cross our legs and refuse to budge if He is challenging our direction, thinking or relationships. I have seen people pray for God to lift them in their 'Now What?' but, when being lifted means accepting correction or surrendering control, they adopt a posture that resists His lift. It's as if they folded their arms to say, 'I won't change! I don't want to take that advice!' When this happens, a spiritual lockdown occurs and they miss out on the purpose God has for them. The people Ezekiel was trying to reach were difficult to get off the ground. Their spiritual stubbornness made them like an immovable weight and their refusal to be lifted restricted their future.

Belly Time

Jonah was another of God's people who at times found it hard to accept the God grab and direction for his destiny. He refused to be lifted to see what God saw about the people of Nineveh. God had compassion towards them, but Jonah's prejudice caused him to go the opposite direction. He allowed his own feelings rather than God's perspective to shape his choices. Jonah was in need of a posture adjustment so God took him to a place where he knew that would happen, the belly of a huge whale. It was during the grab that Jonah's poor posture was addressed as God took him on a journey from rebellion to repentance and from selfishness to surrender. After the lift he was ready to be set back down in Nineveh to deliver his prophetic 'coming soon', the word of hope and deliverance that God had given him.

I think I'd prefer to keep an open posture and build a liftable life than to go through an experience like Jonah's. I know that on several occasions God has needed to place me in a time-out while I adjusted my life. I'm just glad I didn't end up in a fish! So, let's take a look at some of the ways we can improve our internal posture so that God can grab hold of us and lift our lives.

The Prayer Lift

Prayer can help you to adopt an open posture and make it easy for you to be lifted. People sometimes ask me how often they should pray and want to know what my prayer life is like. I always tell them that prayer is a language, it's a constant conversation with God, not a set formula.

Taking up a posture of prayer means that we are open to what God wants to show us. It gets you a step ahead and helps you live life in a way that makes it easy for you to be lifted. Prayer should be a natural part of our lives, so that it becomes effortless. You pray as you go through your day, 'God, I pray my children have a great day at school. I pray that I can help my colleague at work who is depressed. I pray that you would bless that parent in the playground who is going through a difficult divorce - God, help me get alongside her.' When you increase your fluency and become used to praying you adopt a posture in life that makes it easy for God to speak to you about your life.

Prayer is such an intimate part of our relationship with God. It's our time to converse and to share our heart, dreams, and love for him. Prayer keeps our posture flexible. I remember a really hard season in ministry when I felt like I was in the middle of a constant battle. I was weary of people and even got tired of being around church. I remember realising that

I had to find a way to fix myself and prayer became a big part of my breakthrough. I took my internal posture to a spiritual exercise class. I unfolded my tense battle weary arms, I opened my heart that was shut because of the fear of being wounded and I talked with God. I prayed all day no matter whether I was out for a run, driving or even doing the laundry. When I felt tension creep back into my heart I talked to God some more. Prayer made me easy to lift in the midst of circumstances that tried to keep me down. I avoided conflicts as he lifted me over them. I resisted retaliation as he lifted me higher. I believe in the 'Now What?' seasons we must make sure our prayer language is not desperate and frantic but naturally flowing and devotional. Don't wait until a 'Now What?' moment hits to become fluent in the language of prayer. We need to build a prayer life that flows from a place of devotion, not desperation.

In 'Now What?' moments no matter what you face, stay open to His lift. Let your arms stay raised to heaven. Don't let bitterness lock you down, offence sink you or weariness keep you from raising you arms to reach out to Him. Prayer will help you to be pliable and keep an open posture.

The Faith Lift

In many 'Now What?' moments our faith is put to the test and we need to see past the problem and lift our level of expectancy.

Even Ezekiel struggled with this when he was faced with people who ignored the many messages he brought to them from God. Having faith and expectancy for what God can do in every situation is vital if we want our lives to be lifted.

When our son was five, he went through a difficult time at school. He would get upset when he left for school each morning and came home even more upset. He was being bullied by some of the other kids and was carrying too much negativity about what was happening for someone so young. I decided to try and lift him as much as I could each morning before school to help him feel better about the day ahead. Steve and I committed to speak more positive words over him than the negative words the bullies would use when we were not with him. We created an environment that would help to lift him by turning off the cartoons he would sometimes watch before school and replacing them with conversations that would set him up for a great day. We decided that if the first thing our children heard from us in a morning was 'you're going to have an awesome day today,' it would lift them and encourage them to expect that something different was going to happen. We began to lift Noah by encouraging him, telling him he was brilliant and saying, 'Noah – good things happen when you do good!' It became the new catchphrase in our home. We simply wanted to build a new expectancy in his life that the situation he faced would improve.

Within a few weeks we had seen real change; he won two Head Teacher's awards and was presented with a golden medal for good behaviour in front of all the other pupils. It didn't stop there, he received a present through the post that he wasn't expecting and got invited to three parties all in the same day. Afterwards he turned to me and said, ' I get it Mum. Good things happen when you're good!' He learned to expect good things in his life and it added a new positive perspective to his outlook. It lifted his life. Sometimes as adults we need to have the same simple revelation all over again. We need to lift our level of faith and expect good things from God.

The Worship Lift

Worship is another way we can be lifted. I have done some of my best tears at church on the front row in worship. There is something so healing about being in an atmosphere of worship where we allow ourselves to be vulnerable, to be held by him, to fall at his feet and place our agendas aside to adore him. Worship lifts us as we lift him up.

I love the way the Bible describes worshipers. It says 'My question: what are God worshipers like? Your answer: Arrows aimed at God's bulls-eye. They settle down in a promising place; their kids inherit a prosperous farm. God-friendship is for God-worshipers, they are the ones He confides in.' (Psalm 25:12 -14 MSG)

Worship is about surrender, it is about taking up a position where you acknowledge God's greatness and his power. This attitude makes us easy to lift because we are alert and listening intently to what God is saying. Maybe you need to put this book down right now and go and put on a worship CD and just worship. I guarantee you it will lift you, revive you and you will begin to hear God in a new way in your 'Now What?' moment.

Back Down to Earth

God grabs you to give you a preview of what comes next. He lifts you to prepare you for the part you are going to play in his forthcoming features. But God always lifts our lives in order to set us back down. This happened to Ezekiel and I'm sure he was surprised to see where he ended up. He was set back down in a valley full of very dry bones. You may find that after God lifts you He sets you back down amongst the bones of your 'Now What?' moments. But this wasn't the end of Ezekiel's encounter and it won't be the end of yours. Ezekiel was about to see the most thrilling 'coming soon' trailer of his life. So my friend, watch the trailers, let God grab and lift you and then get ready to re-enter your valley.

Now What?

Tips For The God Grab

1. Embrace the 'coming soon', God has a showreel of hope for your life.

2. Prepare your heart for God to grab you and adjust your posture.

3. Don't run from challenge, turn to God and prepare to take responsibility.

4. Get ready for the lift – you can lift your prayer life, faith and worship.

5. What goes up must come down – God will set you back down in the bones of your circumstances, but change is coming.

"God asked Ezekiel, "Can these bones live?" He wants to ask you the same question. Too often we see bones where God sees an army."

Chapter 7

Own Your Bones

After he experienced his God grab, Ezekiel was lifted up and then set back down. Too often in 'Now What?' moments when God lifts us we pray He sets us down in a new place; far away from the problems we hope to escape from. On several occasions I have prayed to God as if He was Captain Kirk from the Starship Enterprise, asking him to 'beam me up' out of a difficult circumstance. I figured it was worth asking; He once did it for the disciple Philip so maybe He would do it for me.

But God is not in the business of transporting His people away from their challenges; He is in the business of standing alongside them so that their test can become a testimony. He didn't beam Daniel up out of the lion's den, He just made the lion's back into a furry pillow for him. Neither did He rescue Shadrach, Meshach and Abednego out of the flames, instead He joined them for a walk in their fiery furnace. We need to have the revelation that sometimes our prayers are contrary to how God works. He doesn't want you to look for some kind of spiritual escapism, He wants to give you the spiritual equipment you need to stand firm and navigate the situations you face.

Back and Forth

God grabbed Ezekiel so He could set him down in a valley of dry bones which was a picture of the broken, desolate lives of God's people.

'God grabbed me. God's Spirit took me up and set me down in the middle of an open plain strewn with bones. He led me around and among them – a lot of bones! There were bones all over the plain – dry bones, bleached by the sun.' (Ezekiel 37:1-2 MSG)

God wanted Ezekiel to face the dry bones of the people he was called to reach. He wanted him to see their lack and brokenness by walking back and forth among the desolate landscape. God also wants us to take a walk in our valleys, to face the dry bones in our lives and refuse to be afraid of seeing our brokenness.

Often we don't want to look at our lack, we want to hide it away. We pray silently to God about our problems but don't want others to know we are in a valley of confusion or see the bare, brittle condition of our lives. If we are too embarrassed or too proud to display our bones, we can end up behaving like my dog, Jake. When he has a bone he immediately takes it out of everyone else's sight. He finds a spot at the far end of our garden to hide it because he doesn't want anyone to come near his secret possession.

We can deal with our failures and problems in the same way. We remove them from sight and dig a hole in our heart to bury them in, hoping that no one notices they exist.

Sadly, I have seen how this behaviour doesn't solve anything. I have been shocked at times to see couples who seemed to be happily married separate. They had hidden the bones of their dysfunctional relationship and by the time they finally decided to own up to them, it was too late. They may have thought they were doing the right thing by ignoring and covering up the ugly dry bones in their life, but in doing so they created a graveyard for their relationship. We have to face facts. If the ministry is not working, if we have failed or if an area of our life has become like a dried up old bone, hiding it will only cause more harm.

God's Question

When God shows you bones it's for a reason. He isn't trying to freak you out or make you feel bad that there are some things in your life that need attention. God took Ezekiel to the valley of bones because He was to going to restore them but the process began with a question for him to answer.

'He said to me, "Son of man, can these bones live?" I said, "Master God, only you know that"' (Ezekial 37:3 MSG)

God already knew the answer to this question. He can make anything live; He can bring the driest bone back to life and isn't phased by situations that look impossible to revive. He asked the question to gauge where Ezekiel's faith was at when faced with such barrenness. God wanted to know whether Ezekiel could see past the problem to the potential. He could see an army in the bones and wanted to know if Ezekiel could see it too.

In our most desperate 'Now What?' moments God wants us to answer the same question. As you walk among the bones of your marriage, ministry, wayward children or broken dreams, he wants to ask you, 'Can these bones live?' Our answer will reveal where our faith is at in the valley.

Ezekiel didn't give a direct response, he deflected the question back to God. As a pastor I have often seen this happen. People bring their bones and want someone else to tell them if they can be fixed. We can't keep avoiding our responsibility to answer God's question and show what we really believe about our situation. Your reply will lead you to God's answer, which as Ezekiel was about to find out, requires your involvement.

The Miracle in Your Mouth

The miracle Ezekiel was about to witness started with his own mouth. Incredible as it seems, when you are in the valley God wants to use the same mouth that you used to say 'Now What?' to solve the problem.

God gave Ezekiel clear instructions of what to do next saying, "Prophesy to these bones and say to them, 'Dry bones, hear the word of the Lord! This is what the Sovereign Lord says to these bones: I will make breath enter you, and you will come to life. I will attach tendons to you and make flesh come upon you and cover you with skin; I will put breath in you, and you will come to life. Then you will know that I am the Lord.'" (Ezekiel 37:4-6)

The Bible talks a lot about the power of the tongue. Our speech is not neutral and often in our 'Now What?' moments we forget the power we possess in our own mouths. We let hopelessness control our conversations and desperation direct our tongue. This causes more damage than we realise. 'The tongue has the power of life or death', or as The Message translation puts it, 'Words kill, words give life.' (Proverbs 18 MSG)

Ezekiel was instructed to kick start the miracle in the valley with his own words by talking to the bones about their future and declaring they would live. Instead of focusing on what he could see he prophesied about what lay ahead in the future. He didn't speak of their deadness but spoke about the life and breath that would enter them. In our times of testing we have to become wise stewards of our words. Don't speak negatively and talk about how dry your bones are or how hopeless the situation looks. Prophesy about the life and breath that can come back into them.

So, let me ask, what words are you speaking over the bones in your life today? Are you saying, 'This relationship is over, we will never find a way forward', or are you saying, 'We are going to believe the best of one another and make a way forward?' Are you confessing financial failure or speaking financial favour? It may seem like such a small thing but we often overlook this key part of our breakthrough. Don't undervalue the importance of your speech. Your mouth is a weapon, so use it wisely to reaffirm God's promises instead of to reinforce your problems.

Life-giving Words

My husband is an amazing man of God, and one of the many things I love about him is that he is someone who always speaks life. He's known and loved by many for his gift of encouragement. I have learnt so much from watching how careful he is with his words. When he first moved to the UK he struggled to understand why people here often see the negative in situations rather than the positive. I love how he refused to surrender to that culture and instead began to challenge the confession of those around him. He would help me with the words I spoke over my own life. When I was negative and claimed it was my British culture to speak that way he would say, 'Well it isn't kingdom culture and it won't help.' Steve continually challenges me to speak life over my bones and in 'Now What?' moments he always pulls out a testimony of hope to remind me how our trial can be used to help others. If we are facing a time of barrenness he will always be the first to start to sing. His prophetic words of life have resurrected so many dreams in my heart and he has breathed life over the dry bones in the lives of many others. He has released countless young people who were told they couldn't succeed, to dream again through our youth ministry. His words have ministered life to older people who thought their best days were over and rekindled their excitement about the life that remains in their bones. I have seen first hand the way we can bring bones to life and how the miracle can start in our own mouth.

In our 'Now What?' moments we need to be willing to look at the bones and to prophesy to the breath, just as God instructed Ezekiel.

Called for Connection

Speaking life was just the beginning; God had more instructions for Ezekiel about what to prophesy. It was time for the bones to get connected with tendons and be covered with skin.

The fact is, a disconnected bone can never be an army on its own. It needs to be connected to the rest of the body. Yet, when we are in our valleys we can end up being disconnected and our lack of relationship can delay our recovery.

Isolation is the enemy's plan to divide what God intended to be united. We must be aware that 'Now What?' moments have massive potential to separate and divide us from others. At the very time when we most need support we can become disconnected; in the seasons when we most need wisdom from others, our pride can keep us independent and alone. In the picture God showed Ezekiel, the bones began to reconnect. They had to reattach to each other so that the dry bones could become part of a living body.

Piece or Big Picture

Walking through a valley can be a lonely experience. In 'Now What?' moments, as you look at the dry bones in your life it is easy to feel insignificant and to think that no one needs you. Insignificance will persuade you that you have nothing worth giving, so why try? We need to understand that our significance comes when we realise we were created to be part of God's big picture. Our piece is supposed to be attached to others, it was never meant to remain alone.

If you ever take the time to complete a jigsaw puzzle there is nothing more annoying than almost getting to the end of the puzzle to discover a piece is missing. You end up searching all over the house for that one small piece. You will lift furniture and even go to the lengths of interrogating your children and looking in the dog's mouth in the hope of retrieving it. When that piece was scattered on the table with thousands of others it didn't seem important, but once you fit the rest of the jigsaw together you start to appreciate the value of the missing piece. In 'Now What?' moments when we are faced with our own dry bones and inadequacies, we can feel we don't measure up and think our piece is surplus to requirements. The fact is, we will never truly understand the significance of our piece unless we see where it fits on God's box lid. When you realise that God intends for your lonely dry bone to become part of an army, it starts to give you a picture of a life that is bigger than just you. When God lifts you it helps you see his box lid picture and you realise that you are not supposed to remain isolated. You must push past your feeling of inadequacy and attach your life to others. Then you will no longer be an isolated bone and your piece will become a useful part.

Significant Sandwiches

The Bible is full of examples of how every piece is needed to complete the picture. Just think about Joseph's story; he was destined to be part of God's big picture and play a leading role as the future Prime Minister. When God first showed Joseph the part he would play as a teenager, it wasn't well received by the other pieces of his family. His brothers let it make them feel insignificant. Instead of seeing that every piece of the picture was necessary they allowed it to divide their family and sold Joseph into slavery. Wrong thinking can prevent us from finding our place in the body. We end up despising our piece and want someone else's instead. This can cause us to lose sight of the important purpose God has for our piece.

Years later when Joseph was wrongly imprisoned, God needed to use another piece to help reconnect him to his destiny. But when the cupbearer was asked to play his part by mentioning Joseph's name to Pharaoh, he forgot. It seems like such a small insignificant piece to mention a guy's name to Pharaoh, but it was a vital part of the big picture. It's loss delayed Joseph's release. We need to understand that everyone's part is significant from the brother to the cupbearer.

What if one young boy's mother had said, 'I don't want to make a sandwich for my son today, it's such an insignificant job'. Then her boy wouldn't have taken a fish sandwich to eat as he listened to Jesus teach. If he had thought his sandwich was an insignificant piece he wouldn't have bothered offering it as a potential solution to feed a hungry crowd. The mother and her son both gave the piece they had even though it seemed small and they became part of something much bigger.

The Sound

Ezekiel was commanded to prophesy to the bones to bring them back to life. When all the parts began to attach a new sound began to be heard. Ezekiel described what happened saying, 'I prophesied just as I'd been commanded. As I prophesied, there was a sound, and oh, rustling! The bones moved and came together, bone to bone. I kept watching. Sinews formed, then muscles on the bones, then skin stretched over them. But they had no breath in them.' (Ezekial 37:7-8)

When we follow the process of reconnecting, we will start to hear a rustling. Your life will begin to have a different sound about it that will replace the sound of stress, worry or panic that can come in our 'Now What?' moment. A rustling sound of hope and faith will let you know that God is restoring life to your bones.

Some Bible commentaries say that the rustling sound Ezekiel could hear was probably the sound of the angels' wings rubbing together as they got busy helping to create bodies out of the pile of dry bones. I love that thought because I know that when we rise up God always sends assistance. We are never alone in our valleys.

Ezekiel's co-operation was key in transforming the valley from a scene of desolation to a picture of strength and hope. We need to prophesy to all the different pieces, 'attach and play your part' and refuse to allow our personal problems to isolate us from God's eternal promises and plans.

Army Arise

God finally told Ezekiel to prophesy to the breath. To speak again to the four winds so that they would breathe life together. This was the moment when the army came to life. 'So I prophesied, just as he commanded me. The breath entered them and they came alive! They stood up on their feet, a huge army.' (Ezekiel 37:10)

God saw an army in the bones from the beginning; it didn't come to life through a quick God intervention, it came to life as Ezekiel followed a prophetic process. In 'Now What?' moments we must be willing to be grabbed, lifted and set down to face our bones just like Ezekiel. Committing to the same process will help us to find hope in the most hopeless of circumstances.

I want you to know that your piece is a vital part of a much bigger picture. Don't allow yourself to become isolated but reattach your life to others. Choose your words carefully when you are faced with a valley experience; use your breath to speak life and not to over analyse your circumstances.

If we will follow the same process as Ezekiel, I believe that our dry bones will find each other. Together we will help to bring increase to the army of God and bring life to what was once a spiritual graveyard. Your 'Now What?' moments don't have to end in a valley of bones. They are an opportunity for our bones to be brought back to life; for us to get a new understanding of where we fit in God's big picture and make the relational attachments we need for our journey.

Now What?

Tips To Own Your Bones

1. God doesn't lift you out of your circumstances but He stands alongside you in them.

2. God wants you to answer the question, 'Can these bones live?'

3. Activate the miracle that's already in your mouth

4. Don't allow 'Now What?' moments to isolate you – get yourself connected to the body.

5. Your bones can become an army if you work with God's prophetic process.

"If God's answer doesn't fit your box, lose the box. Don't overlook His provision because you don't like the way it's packaged."

Chapter 8

Zero Gravity Answers

In 'Now What?' moments when we look to God for an answer we can often expect it to arrive in a certain way. But God does not do a multiple-choice response. He will not be confined to the limited list of options you present to him.

'As the heavens are higher than the earth, so are my ways higher than your ways and my thoughts than your thoughts.' (Isaiah 55:9). We need to understand that God doesn't think like us. We think earthly thoughts that are grounded in our experiences and limited human thinking, but when God brings an answer to your world it comes from a different place. His answer isn't contained by the gravitational pull of your circumstances; heaven's response is often a zero gravity answer.

Often when we pray in times of challenge we have already decided what God's reply should be; we even have a time frame within which we expect him to respond. Our frustration and impatience causes our prayer life to become like a shopping list of needs for God the supplier to fulfil. In 'Now What?'

moments we can move from listening to Jesus to giving Him orders. Instead of serving Him, we serve Him notice of our demands. In these times we must refocus on the name we are calling on. It requires us to step back from the suffocating pressures that surround us and look to the majestic King of Kings who we are praying to. The God we are seeking is our creator so we need to accept that his answers may not have been created yet. He is able to provide bespoke solutions for every situation and is not stuck for an answer even when we are.

God wants us to have a belief system that is big enough to embrace answers we may never have heard of. He is looking for people like Noah - who will accept the seemingly ridiculous answer when it arrives in their world. Noah didn't just have to accept God's zero gravity response, he had to build it. He had no concept of what a flood was and no idea what an ark looked like. Neither did he have a plan for how he would round up two of every kind of animal to put in it. God's answer to the coming flood was definitely zero gravity and Noah had to lose the logical arguments of why this made no sense. He had to trust the God who was above his reasoning and comprehension. Can you imagine how difficult it must have been for Noah to understand what on earth was going on when God said 'Noah, I want you to build me a boat.' Noah must have been very puzzled and replied, 'What's a boat?' God then went on to explain that it was for him to live in when it rained and he flooded the earth. 'What's rain?' asked Noah.

This was just the start of their zero gravity conversation; they hadn't even got to the bit about the animals coming in two by two.

There is no logical explanation for God's request. At times like this the question you only have to ask is, 'Do I trust God or not?' If you do then you must grab a hammer and become a part of the answer. Noah spent years building an ark and waiting for this thing called rain to arrive. Before he had seen a single raindrop he was willing to turn the ark into a floating zoo. I love how Noah just accepted that God has different ways of thinking; it made him open to accepting a zero gravity answer. If your walk with God has become predictable you need to stretch your faith and embrace some out of the box God answers. Be open to hearing him whisper things into your spirit that were never an option on your list. In 'Now What?' moments we need to become more receptive to answers that may not even be on our radar yet.

A Different Approach

When our daughter was about two years old, she developed a fascination with car keys. Steve has always had a tendency to lose his keys, so when they started to go missing around the house I blamed him. Eventually it dawned on me that the real culprit was Hope. She had been taking the keys and hiding them from us. So, I set of on a hunt around the house looking for our lost keys. I looked everywhere I could think of. I suddenly realised that my search was futile because I was looking in the places where I might leave my keys; the top of the fridge, book shelves and bathroom cabinets. I needed to enter her way of thinking and look for places she could reach or would see as attractive hiding spots. With this revelation I got down on my knees and started to consider how she would see the world. As I knelt down in her playroom I spotted a toy car and my search was over. I found all three missing sets of keys hidden inside it.

Often we do the same, we look in all the predictable places for God's solution instead of entering his higher way of thinking. But God leaves answers in some places you would never dream of looking. He isn't predictable, he isn't routine and he doesn't leave his answers on the same shelf that you throw your keys on every day. He is the God whose answer to a financial need on one occasion was to send a coin in a fish's mouth. When an enemy needed defeating the answer once arrived through making a few laps of the city walls and blowing a trumpet. His zero gravity answers are highly creative and often we don't see them coming. The good news is, neither does the enemy.

Sledgehammer Thinking

A few years ago my parents bought a new baby grand piano. The room they wanted to put it in was up some stairs and around a corner so the guy from the piano shop came to measure the space to make sure it would fit. The day it was delivered my Dad and a few of the guys from church who came to help him tried to move the piano, but although they could get it upstairs, they couldn't manoeuvre it around the corner. It was a tricky situation and a few of them started to panic in case they dropped it because it was very heavy. At that moment a zero gravity thought came into my Dad's head and he asked if anyone had a sledge hammer. He proceeded to smash the doorframe until the gap was wide enough for them to get the piano into the room. Most people would have put it in a different room and thought, 'why mess up a perfectly neat wall for a piano?' This way of thinking is a reason we can often miss the answer we are praying for. I believe that we have sent back many spiritual piano answers that would have added music to our hearts because we refused to move our walls. We need to be bold enough to take the hammer out and smash our way past our own containment to embrace God's answers. I would rather have an untidy wall than an empty room.

Jesus loved those who were willing to create a mess in order to receive an answer. One man received his healing because his friends were willing to think outside the box to get him to Jesus. They put him on a mat and carried him to Jesus, but when they couldn't get near enough they came up with a creative solution. They climbed onto the roof, dug a big hole through it and lowered their friend down in front of Jesus' feet (Mark 2:1-5). This wasn't a tidy process, they made a lot of mess and created a big disturbance. But their novel approach got Jesus' attention and their friend received his miracle. Others that day stood in line for hours waiting for their healing and probably didn't even get to Jesus. Sometimes to reach our answer we must smash some walls, lower some mats and line up our thinking with God's.

Spit and Dip

A deaf man wanted his healing from Jesus. Yet it came in a most unusual and unorthodox way. 'Some people brought a man who could neither hear or speak and asked Jesus to lay a healing hand on him. He took the man off by himself, put his fingers in the man's ears and some spit on the man's tongue. Then Jesus looked up in prayer, groaned mightily, and commanded, "Ephphatha!" – "Open up!" And it happened. The man's hearing was clear and his speech plain – just like that.' (Mark 7:31-37)

I don't know if that man was ready for the answer that came his way that day. I doubt he was expecting Jesus to spit on him and stick his fingers in his ears. The friends of the deaf man had already decided what their answer would look like. They didn't just want Jesus to heal him, they wanted it doing in a certain way and asked 'Can you lay your hands on him?' They expected Jesus to heal their friend in the same way he had healed many others. I'm sure they didn't expect that Jesus' zero gravity answer would involve spitting.

The Bible tells of other occasions when people were healed or received their answers in ways that challenged their thinking. Elisha sent a message to a man called Naaman who had leprosy. He instructed him to go and wash in a dirty river seven times to be healed. It was an answer that could have worsened his skin condition instead of improving it and at first he refused to accept this unconventional approach.

'So Naaman with his horses and chariots arrived in style and stopped at Elisha's door. Elisha sent out a servant to meet him with this message: "Go to the River Jordan and immerse yourself seven times. Your skin will be healed and you'll be as good as new." Naaman lost his temper. He turned on his heel saying, "I thought he'd personally come out and meet me, call on the name of God, wave his hand over the diseased spot, and get rid of the disease. The Damascus rivers, Abana and Pharpar, are cleaner by far than any of the rivers in Israel. Why not bathe in them? I'd at least get clean." He stomped off, mad as a hornet. But his servants caught up with him and said, "Father, if the prophet had asked you to do something hard and heroic, wouldn't you have done it? So why not this simple 'wash and be clean?'

So he did it. He went down and immersed himself in the Jordan seven times, following the orders of the Holy Man. His skin was healed; it was like the skin of a little baby. He was as good as new.' (2 Kings 5:1-14 MSG)

This wasn't just about Naaman's skin; it was also about his pride. He was expecting his answer to look far grander and more exciting than a dirty bath; he wanted a personal visit from the prophet. But unless he had finally humbled himself and got into the dirty water he wouldn't have received his miracle of clean skin. Dipping in dirty water might not sound attractive but if that's God's answer, deal with your pride and go dip.

I want to ask you a question. Can God spit on you? Can He stick his fingers in your ears if that is what it will take? Can He do whatever He wants to do to bring the answer you're looking for? Can you lose the job you're praying to keep if that's the answer? Can you move house, end that relationship or sow the money He told you to give? How open are we in our 'Now What?' moments to some zero gravity answers.

Adding Needs

The widow from Zarephath is a beautiful illustration of how God's answers can work. It was a time of drought and severe famine, and Elijah was camping near to the Jordan River. He needed a miracle of provison and God's first zero gravity answer was to send ravens to bring him meat to eat each day. His answer was made even more miraculous by the fact that ravens are meat-eating birds. For the ravens to deliver meat without eating it required them to curb their carnivorous nature. When the brook he was drinking from dried up, God moved his answer to another town and told Elijah to travel to Zarephath. His next answer was to be found in a town he was unfamiliar with and come from a woman who was already in great need.

'So he went to Zarephath. When he came to the town gate, a widow was there gathering sticks. He called to her and asked, "Would you bring me a little water in a jar so I may have a drink?" As she was going to get it, he called, "And bring me, please, a piece of bread."

"As surely as the Lord your God lives," she replied, "I don't have any bread – only a handful of flour in a jar and a little olive oil in a jug. I am gathering a few sticks to take home and make a meal for myself and my son, that we may eat it – and die."' (1 Kings 17 7-12)

This widow was experiencing her own 'Now What?' moment. She was about to eat her last meal with her son before they died and God sent her another mouth to feed. She needed provision and God sent her need; Elijah needed supplies and God sent him to someone who had no resources. This is how zero gravity answers often work; they can appear to make the situation worse. We have to understand that God can see the big picture; he will not provide us with a quick-fix temporary answer when he knows we actually need a long-term approach.

The widow's meeting with Elijah placed a demand on her life. Responding to it was costly and meant giving up some of the little precious food she had that could have fed her son. It requires a deep trust in God to give something away that is costly before you can see your answer. It wasn't an easy decision, the widow was fearful of her present trials, but her willingness to co-operate with God secured her future triumph.

Elijah said to her, "Don't be afraid. Go home and do as you have said. But first make a small loaf of bread for me from what you have and bring it to me, and then make something for yourself and your son. For this is what the Lord, the God of Israel, says: "The jar of flour will not be used up and the jug of oil will not run dry until the day the Lord sends rain on the land." (1 Kings 17:13-14)

She went away and did as Elijah had told her. So there was food every day for Elijah and for the woman and her family. For the jar of flour was not used up and the jug of oil did not run dry, in keeping with the word of the Lord spoken by Elijah.' (1 Kings 17:16)

We could think that this was the end of the story; she obeyed God and received her answer. But it was just the beginning; God knew there was a greater need on its way. When the widow's son fell ill and died she experienced the worst 'Now What?' moment any mother could face. She found herself calling out to God in desperation, but by divine design her answer was already in her world. The mouth she had chosen to feed in her time of lack was now going to be the same mouth God would use to breathe life back into her dead son's body.

"Give me your son," Elijah replied. He took him from her arms, carried him to the upper room where he was staying, and laid him on his bed. Then he cried out to the Lord, "Lord my God, have you brought tragedy even on this widow I am staying with, by causing her son to die?" Then he stretched himself out on the boy three times and cried out to the Lord, "Lord my God, let this boy's life return to him!" The Lord heard Elijah's cry, and the boy's life returned to him, and he lived. Elijah picked up the child and carried him down from the room into the house. He gave him to his mother and said, "Look, your son is alive!'" (1 Kings 17:19-23)

God had sent a zero gravity answer into the widow's life that he had prepared in advance. Her solution was right in front of her, she just had to recognise it. Sometimes in 'Now What?' moments we can allow our panic to blind us to God's answers because they look different to how we imagined. We need to learn to trust him and be willing to let him place Elijah's in our world, even when it is costly for us to accept them. It may not make sense to welcome them at the time but later we will see God's perfect plan unfold.

We need to see past the circumstances of our 'Now What?' moments and respond to the demands God's zero gravity answers may place on our life. If God's answer doesn't fit in your box, get a bigger one and expand your thinking. Don't overlook his provision because it wasn't packaged how you'd expected.

God is all seeing, all knowing and all powerful. He wants to send us creative answers but I believe we restrict our ability to receive them by looking for them in the wrong places or asking for wrong things. He knows what you need so if he sends you a prophet to feed when you had asked for a grocery delivery, you'd better get ready to feed Elisha. The zero gravity answer you receive today may well hold the answer you need tomorrow.

Now What?

Tips For Zero Gravity Answers

1. God's thoughts are higher than yours, maybe you need to lift your thinking.

2. Can God spit on you? God's zero gravity answer may be outside your comfort zone.

3. Your answer may place a demand on your life before it arrives.

4. Sometimes the demand placed on you today will become the miracle you need tomorrow.

5. Don't turn away Gods provision because you don't like the way it's packaged.

"On our worst days, when the soil is barren, our friends are gone and trials are relentless, we must still know how to grow our lives."

Chapter 9

Grow Your Own

I remember once teaching a final session with some of our Leadership Academy students as they prepared to graduate. They had spent nine months at the church, serving in different areas and sitting in teaching sessions every day. As I was about to finish I asked if they had any questions. One of them shot their hand up in the air and said, 'what is the best advice you can give us as we finish our time here?'

I responded with an answer that wasn't rehearsed and one that they may have felt was a little disappointing. I said, 'the best advice I can give you is to discover how to grow yourself.'

I was making the point to the students that they had been in the greenhouse environment of our academy for many months. Every morning, whether they liked it or not, someone was making them grow by teaching them and suggesting new ways of thinking. They had been planted in the healthy fertile soil of the local church where they had been pruned and watered. They had experienced where it says, 'Planted in the house of the Lord, they will flourish.' (Psalm 92:13)

However, I knew that many of the students were going back into the business world, to university or to pioneer a ministry. They wouldn't have the guarantee of people investing in them every day and I didn't want them to leave the hot house environment they had been thriving in to discover that they hadn't learned to grow their own lives.

Growth by Trial

Our 'Now What?' moments can reveal any gaps in our personal and spiritual growth; they give us a realistic measure of our progress. When the unforeseen happens we find out how tall our tolerance is, how strong our resolve to love is and how high our integrity stands. The trials of life show us the measure of our maturity and the height of our spiritual stature. We need to look within and learn to grow our own life in the middle of the most challenging circumstances.

Job was a servant of God who knew what it was to face 'Now What?' moments that would cause most of us to quit. The challenges he faced caused him to examine what he had grown on his own journey with God. He lost all his familar points of reference; his business, wealth, health and even his own children. At the time when he needed the most support he found his friends to be 'miserable comforters.' Instead of helping him they looked for the sin in Job's life. Even his wife failed to support him and advised Job to 'curse God and die.'

(Job 2:9) Job realised that if he was to make it through this season he would have to dig deep and grow his own life. He found he could grow trust in the trial and sow his own harvest in the most hostile of lands. Job didn't grow and flourish after his trial, he grew during the test and because of that God blessed Jobs' life.

The Bible teaches to 'Consider it pure joy, my brothers whenever you face trials of many kinds, because you know the testing of your faith develops perseverance' (James 1:2-3). Job discovered the truth of this scripture when he used his test to bring forth new treasure in his own life. I believe that in our 'Now What?' moments we need to make the same discovery; that something good can grow in our lives through the hardest of times. James exhorts us to blossom in the middle of the desert; to grow when the circumstances would tell us to shrink back. Our 'Now What?' moments will put a demand on our lives and we need to prepare for it in advance.

I don't want to wait until a 'Now What?' moment to discover that I am lacking in areas where I thought there was a plentiful supply. When I need to draw on my reserve of love; I don't want to discover that my well has dried up. In a time of hostility; I don't want to find that my peace is out of stock. When I am tested relationally; I don't want to be told that my grace has insufficient funds. If we are to grow through every circumstance, then we must commit to keep growing our lives.

Growing Partners

As I mentioned at the outset of chapter one, I love to run; it's a daily discipline in my life. But I have noticed that when I run on my own I usually cover the same number of miles at the same speed each time. However, I often take my good friend Abs with me when I travel to speaking engagements and she also loves running. When we run together something comes over me and I start to show my competitive streak. I try to increase my pace to outrun her and I know she starts to race me too. On those days I go further and faster than when I run alone; her companionship makes me want to do better. This works the same spiritually because God-centred friends make great growing partners. They are destined by God to be alongside you and push you to grow faster.

The Bible puts it this way, 'As iron sharpens iron, so one person sharpens another' (Proverbs 27:17). If you want to be sharpened and grow, get around some people who will help you. Invest in developing strong friendships with people who have a positive impact on your world. We all need friends or mentors who believe in us, genuinely care for us and even prune us so that more growth can come. 'Wounds from a friend can be trusted' (Proverbs 27:6). We need friends who will help us grow and love us enough to be truthful about our strengths and weaknesses. However, we can't delegate the responsibility of growing our lives to someone else; it starts with us. My friend may push me to run faster but she doesn't make me run. I have to show up at the gym regularly, get on the treadmill and work on improving my stamina. We mustn't misunderstand the place of relationships in growing our lives. Don't be like the person who says, 'I want to get fit,' but then expects their personal trainer to make it happen for them. Initial progress may be made, but unless responsibility is taken for their personal fitness, long-term progress will be unsustainable.

Environmental Growth

Our environment is another key factor in our growth. We need to find fertile soil for our lives and an environment that is rich in faith. However, the soil is not solely responsible for the growth of the plants rooted in it. The plants have to play their part by taking in nutrients and growing a crop for others.

Jesus once cursed a fig tree that wouldn't grow because it was violating an important principle. The tree was taking the goodness from the soil and producing nothing in return. Jesus knew that there were figs inside the tree, but it was withholding its fruit. He wouldn't have cursed it if the ground had been barren; he wouldn't have demanded fruit if the soil was poor, but the environment was favourable for growth (Mark 11:20). God wants you to plant your life in fertile soil and will hold you to account for the fruit you produce. Too often I have seen people leave churches declaring that there was a problem with the quality of the soil while the life next to them was flourishing in the same conditions. The fig tree was the problem not the soil and if we want to keep growing and produce a great crop, we need to be willing to yield our fruit.

There are many different things that can help to grow our lives but none can take the place of growing it ourselves. On our worst days when the soil is barren, our friends are gone and the trials are relentless, we must still know how to grow.

Grow Yourself

Jesus' growth as a young man was deliberate and by design. He took responsibility for growing His own life because He knew that one day He would be used to grow the lives of others. I love how His hunger for growth even confused those who were closest to Him. It caused Him to be a very different child. While most kids His age would be hanging out at the park or playing games in the street; Jesus could be found in the temple absorbing God's word and growing His life. It even records how Jesus' parents once lost him; I'm sure it was embarrassing for them to admit they had misplaced the Messiah. They were travelling together as a family when Jesus took an unplanned detour to the temple. After looking in all the usual places that a twelve year old might go, they eventually found him sat listening to the teachers of the law. (Luke 12:41-50) Jesus had a commitment to grow his own life and knew He couldn't rely on his natural parents to prepare Him for His supernatural calling. He was aware that He would be responsible for growing the lives of others and you have to grow yourself before you can grow someone else.

God's word brings growth. 'My son, if you accept my words and if you store up my commands within you, turning your ear to wisdom and applying your heart to understanding, and if you look for it as silver and search for it as hidden treasure, then you will understand the fear of the Lord and find the knowledge of God' (Proverbs 2:1-2) These verses talk about you turning your ear, not someone dragging you to wisdom or forcing it on you. It goes on to talk about searching for it as if it was silver. It's clear that we need to develop a strong desire to grow.

I remember once losing my diamond engagement ring. I had left it on the kitchen unit, but when I went to put it back on my hand it was gone. I immediately instigated a search party; I got on my knees going through garbage bags looking desperately for my missing diamond. After looking through chicken carcasses and empty cereal packets I finally found my treasure in the trash. I wonder if we are desperate enough for wisdom that we would search through every garbage bag, every hardship and every test to find it. Have you ever searched for a way to grow your life as if you were searching for hidden treasure? Have you ever turned your heart upside down hunting for a way to improve the bad attitude that has kept you small? Growth takes effort; you must search for it as if you had lost something valuable.

I am on a journey of growing my life just like you and I want to share three growth tips with you that help me to grow.

Place a Demand

I have noticed that there are two different kinds of people in life; those who are demanding of others, and those who put a demand on themselves. Demanding people often look to others to grow their life, they don't have a work ethic that involves growing their own. I believe God is looking for us to put a demand on what He has already placed inside of us. 'His divine power has given us everything we need for a Godly life through our knowledge of him...' (2 Peter 1:3). We already have everything we need; maybe it's just time for us to start placing more of a demand on it.

Are you doing anything that places a demand on the power already inside you? Are you daring to be more adventurous, to step out or speak up? We can have an ocean of power and yet only draw a few drops from it. We need to ask bigger, dream greater and release the potential that is already within us. Until you start to do this you will never know what you can achieve and overcome in life.

If we look again into the life of Joseph, we find he understood what it meant to place a demand on himself. He was falsely accused of assaulting his boss's wife and thrown in jail. He had a choice; to give up and let it ruin his life, or to place a demand on what was inside him. I'm sure it was far from easy. While he was in prison he had to demand that he would keep a right attitude; he had to demand that he would keep his thinking right about the things of God without letting bitterness damage his heart. Joseph didn't let prison contain him or false allegations confine him. He kept growing by demanding more from his heart. That's why, when the demand was placed on his life to lead a nation and save them from famine, he was ready. His life had been stretched and grown through his commitment to keep searching for treasure in the dungeon of his circumstances. He may have been physically imprisoned, but it was no barrier to his growth on the inside.

The apostle Paul was someone who also understood this. With a life full of beatings, shipwrecks and spells in jail, he knew how to place a demand on himself. I love how when it was time for Paul to advise his young disciple Timothy, he passed on the knowledge that he had used to grow his own life. He urged Timothy to grow himself; to be 'prepared in season and out' and to have a strong ethic of growth in his personal life.

He told Timothy on one occasion, 'Don't let anyone look down on you because you are young, but set an example for the believers in speech, in conduct, in love, in faith and in purity. Until I come, devote yourself to the public reading of Scripture, to preaching and to teaching. Do not neglect your gift, which was given you through prophecy when the body of elders laid their hands on you. Be diligent in these matters; give yourself wholly to them, so that everyone may see your progress. Watch your life and doctrine closely. Persevere in them, because if you do, you will save both yourself and your hearers.' (1 Timothy 4:11-16)

These instructions to Timothy are a formula for growth. Real growth can only come when you devote yourself, study the word and be disciplined on your own journey.

I decided many years ago that I would be the most demanding person in my own life. I have chosen to put the demand on me to grow up; to demand a bigger capacity from my own heart before I ask for it from anyone else. I want to make a demand on every gift I have been given. To be honest, it can be hard work at times. It takes effort to change, to handle that situation better, to love people when they let you down and to grow your faith through your failings.

Maybe you have neglected what's on the inside of you. You think that there is nothing there or that you can't grow. I want you to know that there is plenty inside of you. Maybe you just need to put a demand on it and connect yourself to all that God has deposited in your life. Don't rely on others for resources and answers that you could draw from your own life as you place a demand on the gift God has placed in you.

Auto-Correct Your Life

Have you ever had a mobile phone with predictive text? As you type a word, the phone changes it automatically if it thinks you have spelt it wrong. It may sound like a good idea, but it can be very annoying when it corrects it to the wrong word! But most of the time it is more help than hindrance. This auto-correction facility is built into the programming. It is constantly on alert, checking for mistakes and correcting them as they happen. If we are going to grow our own lives we have to install an auto-correct facility in our faith. It means that you are willing to sit yourself down and change when you make a mistake instead of waiting for someone else to point it out to you. I have found that auto-correction is one of the best ways to grow.

Easy or Hard?

Have you ever heard someone say, 'You can learn the easy way or the hard way?' I have said these words to my children on many occasions when I have urged them to do what I had asked. However, more often than not they would rather ignore the first three warnings and learn the hard way. Their stubbornness causes their journey to be more painful and drawn out than necessary. They needed to learn something important but it was their decision whether they did it the easy or the hard way.

I think some of us have this mentality about the things of God; we choose to learn the hard way. Someone has to sit us down to talk about our attitude, or we reach a crisis situation before we take the hint that we need to change. Often we could avoid many painful correction moments if we had learnt to auto-correct. Sometimes you can watch someone making a mess and think, 'If only you had auto-corrected you could have avoided this.'

I remember early on in ministry having too many painful, self-inflicted sit-downs. Eventually I realised that the only person who had got me into those situations was the same person who could get me out of them - me! I could have avoided tantrums and tears if I had chosen the easy way and said to myself, 'Charlotte, you know that's wrong, so why are you waiting for three people to point it out to you?'

We can learn the easy way by auto-correcting our lives, or choose the hard way and learn through our stubbornness and mistakes. One hurts more than the other but both can grow you. Like a good parent, God wants all of the circumstances you face to grow you, but you get to choose whether your learning is easy or hard.

Putting Things Right

Jesus loved people who had an auto-correct facility. He didn't have to do a long sit down and tell them what was wrong with their life. They just got on with correcting their own lives and changing their behaviour.

I love the story of Zacchaeus. He was someone who had an inbuilt auto-correction facility and it transformed his life. 'Jesus entered Jericho and was passing through. A man was there by the name of Zacchaeus; he was a chief tax collector and was wealthy. He wanted to see who Jesus was, but because he was short he could not see over the crowd. So he ran ahead and climbed a sycamore-fig tree to see him, since Jesus was coming that way. When Jesus reached the spot, he looked up and said to him, "Zacchaeus, come down immediately. I must stay at your house today." So he came down at once and welcomed him gladly. All the people saw this and began to mutter, "He has gone to be the guest of a sinner." But Zacchaeus stood up and said to the Lord, "Look, Lord! Here and now I give half of my possessions to the poor, and if I have cheated anybody out of anything, I will pay back four times the amount."' (Luke 19:1-10)

Now What?

Jesus didn't ask for anything from Zacchaeus even though he knew he was a cheat. He didn't give him a good talking to and expose his sin and mistakes. Jesus didn't need to say a single word because Zacchaeus' auto-correct facility kicked in. Just being around Jesus was enough for him to realise that his behaviour was wrong and he instantly offered to pay people back four times the amount he had cheated them of. He didn't need Jesus to tell him to put right his wrongs, he chose to auto-correct his life.

If you want to grow your life, the best advice I can give is for you to learn how to auto-correct. Allow the Holy Spirit to convict you of those areas you need to change and get to work on your life.

In seasons of challenge we all get a true reading of the growth in our lives. Make a fresh commitment today to plant seeds in every season; to irrigate the areas that are dry and till the soil of your heart. Devote yourself to becoming a better gardener. Grow your own harvest so that in your 'Now What?' moments you have a stockpile of supplies.

Now What?

Tips To Grow Your Life

1. Don't rely on others to grow you; learn to grow your own life.

2. Your environment is important; plant your life in good soil where you can flourish.

3. You have everything you need to grow; draw on the deposit God has placed within you.

4. Auto-correct your life, don't wait for others to point out where you need to change.

5. Grow in every season whether feast or famine.

"Greet your trials with a pioneer spirit, however unfamiliar the terrain. Determine that you will navigate a new path. Turn your trial into someone elses trail of hope."

Chapter 10

Limitless

It was a dark night in December and we were having a Christmas dinner party at our house. After the church service ended, I hurried out of the door to get home in time to light all the candles before our guests arrived. As I drove along preoccupied with the evening ahead, I was jolted from my thoughts by a bright light that flashed at me as I went past. I looked in my rearview mirror and realised that a speed camera had taken my picture. In my impatience to get home I'd broken the speed limit. Now I could expect an early Christmas gift to be delivered to my house from the City Council; a speeding fine.

This incident made me more aware of the speed limits near my home and the growing amount of cameras enforcing them. I didn't want to make the same mistake and get another ticket. While this behavioural adjustment is necessary in the natural I have found that the enemy will try to use our 'Now What?' moments to enforce spiritual speed limits in our lives. He sees our mistakes and failures as an opportunity to make us fearful of a fine and warn us against stepping out again. The challenges we face can slow us down and betrayals can put permanent limits on our ability to trust. If we aren't careful, each 'Now What?' moment will be used to set up another spiritual speed restriction to make us over-cautious and frightened to move ahead. We need to wise up to the enemy's plans. He wants to limit your enthusiasm to 40mph and reduce your destiny to 30mph. He wants the church to be made up of leisurely Sunday afternoon drivers who are contained and confined by their past mistakes.

But God doesn't want your 'Now What?' moments to limit you. He wants each wrong restriction in your life to be broken and for you to discover freedom from all containment. Christ came to break every limitation the enemy sought to put on God's people; from the limitation of sin to the restriction of sickness and pain. He came to bring liberty to the prisoners of fear and pierce the limitation of darkness with His light. So be vigilant on your journey. When the enemy tries to erect limitations in your life, remind him that you serve a limitless God, who aims to remove restrictions from people's lives.

'The Spirit of the Sovereign Lord is on me, because the Lord has anointed me to preach good news to the poor. He has sent me to bind up the brokenhearted, to proclaim freedom for the captives and release from darkness for the prisoners, to proclaim the year of the Lord's favour and the day of vengeance of our God, to comfort all who mourn, and provide for those who grieve in Zion - to bestow on them a crown of beauty instead of ashes, the oil of gladness instead of mourning, and a garment of praise instead of a spirit of despair.' (Isaiah 61:1-3)

This scripture holds fast in every 'Now What?' moment we are called to navigate. We have access to an anointing that has the power to remove every restriction the enemy may seek to place on us.

Turnaround God

We serve a limitless God who sees the circumstances we are crying over today as victories already won. He sees the tides we feel are against us as already having turned around. God can look at a rebel called Saul and see in him the apostle Paul. He can look at a frightened man called Gideon and see a warrior in the making. When He looks at you He sees your brokenness as healed and your problems brought to peace. We serve a God who specialises in turnarounds.

'Now What?' moments often seem to be the end of something, we can feel the pain of our loss and feel the futility of our failures. But God's endings always lead us to His new beginnings. He wants to turn your life around, not leave it in a dead end. Yet to turn something around requires our cooperation. Our 'Now What?' moments can often leave us with our heads spinning. The turbulence of the test can cause us to feel we have lost our way but these moments are not just about surviving, they are about surrendering. They are often times when God will not just help us, He will also turn us. These times are as much about refocusing us as they are about fixing us. He wants to recalibrate our thinking, and reprogramme some of our restrictive software.

Update Your GPS

Our car has a global positioning system (GPS), for which I am very thankful as map reading has never been my strength. I have discovered that if we don't update our GPS, we can often end up missing out on new, quicker routes that have been created. In your 'Now What?' moments God wants to update your spiritual GPS. He doesn't want you to keep following the same old route, he wants you to look for the new paths you are supposed to navigate.

I love reading about the prophet Elisha. As a young man he had a turn around encounter with the older prophet Elijah who interrupted his life with an invitation to follow Him. This presented Elisha with a 'Now What?' moment to navigate. He had to choose whether to stay home on a familiar path or follow this crazy prophet on an unknown, unmarked road. 'So Elijah went from there and found Elisha son of Shaphat.

He was ploughing with twelve yoke of oxen, and he himself was driving the twelfth pair. Elijah went up to him and threw his cloak around him. Elisha then left his oxen and ran after Elijah. "Let me kiss my father and mother goodbye," he said, "and then I will come with you."

"Go back," Elijah replied. "What have I done to you?" Elisha then left him and went back. He took his yoke of oxen and slaughtered them. He burned the ploughing equipment to cook the meat and gave it to the people, and they ate. Then he set out to follow Elijah and became his attendant.' (1 Kings 19:19-22)

Elisha realised that in order to navigate this 'Now What?' moment he needed to respond with his future in mind. He had an opportunity to turn his life around but to embrace it he had to close one door so that he could walk through the next. Elisha felt the pull of the future but also the hold of the past; so he took two practical steps to create a path for him to move ahead. First, Elisha burnt his ploughs, which represented his livelihood, the trade that he had always known. But he knew that in this next season he wasn't called to plough, but to prophesy. Elisha wasn't leaving his options open, he was stepping out in faith and removing the restrictions of his past. With no plough there was no back up plan, he wasn't considering doing a u-turn if things didn't work out.

Elisha also closed the door relationally by saying goodbye to his parents because he knew that the road ahead required separation. If he didn't close this door there could have been a relational restriction as he moved forward. He was leaving his natural father and was now going to serve a new spiritual mentor; he had to emotionally detach, to help himself move on. The wise navigational moves he made allowed him to follow Elijah without restrictions or regrets.

Transitional Navigation

'Now What?' moments are often not just a turnaround of circumstances but they are about transitioning from one season to the next. In these times we can be so focused on the door that is opening that we miss the one that needs closing. In our 'Now What?' moments we must look for the right entrance and the exit points so that when we emerge from our challenge we end up on the right road.

Later on in his ministry Elisha had another 'Now What?' transition to navigate. Elijah was going to be taken up to heaven by God and he would be left behind. Elijah was someone he had followed and trusted to give him direction for his life. But Elisha knew that a new time was coming when he would become the giver of directions to others. In this transitional 'Now What?' moment there were many mixed messages that Elisha had to navigate.

'When the Lord was about to take Elijah up to heaven in a whirlwind, Elijah and Elisha were on their way from Gilgal. Elijah said to Elisha, "Stay here; the Lord has sent me to Bethel." But Elisha said, "As surely as the Lord lives and as you live, I will not leave you."' So they went down to Bethel.

The company of the prophets at Bethel came out to Elisha and asked, "Do you know that the Lord is going to take your master from you today?"

"Yes, I know," Elisha replied, "so be quiet."

Then Elijah said to him, "Stay here, Elisha; the Lord has sent me to Jericho."

And he replied, "As surely as the Lord lives and as you live, I will not leave you." So they went to Jericho.

The company of the prophets at Jericho went up to Elisha and asked him, "Do you know that the Lord is going to take your master from you today?"

"Yes, I know,' he replied, 'so be quiet."

Then Elijah said to him, "Stay here; the Lord has sent me to the Jordan."

And he replied, "As surely as the Lord lives and as you live, I will not leave you.' So the two of them walked on." (2 Kings 2:1 -6)

Elisha pushed past the limitation of being told 'no' five times. He refused to let the fear or control of others determine his direction. Elisha held onto God's direction for his life; in this transitional 'Now What?' moment he refused to be restricted and by doing so he inherited a double portion of Elijah's spirit. If we want a double portion anointing we also must have the faith and conviction to navigate our transitions well. If you allow the approval of others to restrict you and cause you to exit your journey too soon, then you may fail to inherit what could have been yours.

Both Elisha and Elijah found themselves caught up in the same transitional moment, but both would exit it in two very different directions. For Elijah it meant taking a chariot ride up to heaven; for Elisha it meant carrying a double portion of anointing down on earth. We must be aware that in 'Now What?' moments people's exit points will often not look the same.

Losing Your Bearings

Later on in Elisha's life he encountered a woman who lost her bearings during a 'Now What?' moment. Her story is one that required a complete turn around. She was widowed, in debt and now in fear for her sons' futures. Faced with her lack she needed to find her way to a limitless God. But in order to navigate her challenge there were several things she had to do which we can learn from. 'The wife of a man from the company of the prophets cried out to Elisha, "Your servant my husband is dead, and you know that he revered the Lord.

But now his creditor is coming to take my two boys as his slaves."' (2 Kings 4:1-7)

This widow's limitation had been pressing in on her for sometime. We don't know how long she had carried this debt and faced this fear alone but eventually in her 'Now What?' moment she came to a place where she had begun to drown in her circumstances. There will be many times when we feel the same sense of desperation and it is in these moments that we must turn our private panic into an audible cry for help.

As children we have no problem with asking when we need an answer. At school we are encouraged to raise our hand if there is something we want to know. Every time we ask, another limitation is lifted from our life; confidence grows and clarity is added to our journey. As adults we are often less willing to ask questions; we let our pride or embarrassment silence us. But in 'Now What?' moments often we keep quiet. We must be willing to ask for directions to find our way out. The widow didn't cry out to a random person for directions, she asked Elisha; a man who she knew was a skilled navigator. In our times of testing we must refrain from crying out to just anyone, but be purposeful about the ones we ask for help. Look for those who have journeyed their path well. Look for those who have feared God more than people and who have pushed past their limitations to carve out new paths. When you cry out, make sure it's in the direction of someone who will help and not hinder your transition.

Look Again

You can often tell if you have called out to the right person by what happens next. If their first response is to comfort you, then that person may be a port of strength in your storm but not necessarily a guide for your path. Elisha's response was one that was going to train this widow. He wasn't going to map the route out for her; he aimed to help her reprogramme her spiritual GPS. He wanted the widow to get her needs met and to be able to navigate her own turn around.
Elisha began with a question: "How can I help you? Tell me, what do you have in your house?" (2 Kings 4:2)

It could be seen as insensitive to ask someone what they have in the middle of their need. She must have thought, 'surely my cry for help was enough to let you know that I have nothing?' But often in the midst of our desperation, God wants to ask us to look again inside our own life. He wants us to examine what we have that could be used to kick-start our miracle with. In your 'Now What?' moments, God wants you to cry for help and to be willing to help yourself. He wants you to look again at what you may have overlooked

I was driving home from my office one day when I noticed a massive sign on a stone wall that said 'reclamation yard.'

When I saw it I was reminded again of how in our 'Now What?' moments we often need to go and look again at things we have discarded. Gifts we have said don't work and dreams we have thrown out believing they are useless. Reclamation yards are full of items that one person wrote off as junk but another saw worth and even beauty in. I remember once watching a programme about people who buy items of furniture from reclamation yards, strip them back, refinish them and sell them on for thousands of pounds. Elisha was urging this widow to do the same. He wanted her to go back to her own reclamation yard and look again at what she had said was empty and useless. He knew that she had something valuable to offer, she just needed to see it.

It wasn't long until she re-emerged from the same pantry that she had previously declared to be empty and announced, 'Your servant has nothing there at all,' she said, "except a small jar of olive oil." (2 Kings 4:2)

From Except to Exceptional

'Except' is a small word but it can make an incredible difference to what happens next in our lives. When we face challenging circumstances we need to look again for our 'except'. Our 'Now What?' moments will often cause us to consider our life to be barren. We can fail to see the 'little oil' as it seems insignificant in the face of such a challenge. This is why we need the ability to look again, to walk through our spiritual reclamation yard and extract every 'except.' When our except meets a limitless God it will soon become exceptional as we are about to see through this woman's life.

The next instruction Elisha gave her is something that would be an even greater stretch. He was now working on reprogramming her restricted faith. He didn't want her to settle for her needs being met, he wanted her to go from having just enough to having more than enough.

'Elisha then added, "Go round and ask all your neighbours for empty jars. Don't ask for just a few. Then go inside and shut the door behind you and your sons. Pour oil into all the jars, and as each is filled, put it to one side."' She left him and shut the door behind her and her sons. They brought the jars to her and she kept pouring. When all the jars were full, she said to her son, "Bring me another one."

But he replied, "There is not a jar left." Then the oil stopped flowing. She went and told the man of God, and he said, "Go, sell the oil and pay your debts. You and your sons can live on what is left."' (2 Kings 4:3-7)

It seems like a strange request to ask a woman who had nothing except a little oil to collect as many empty pots and pans as she could find. But I believe that God wanted to demonstrate his limitless nature to her. She may have had enough faith for just her jar to be filled, but God wanted to demonstrate that he was far greater than her needs and could sustain her and many others with his limitless supply.

God didn't want the widow's miracle to stay inside her own

four walls. It involved her neighbours, friends and whoever was willing to help. Everyone who loaned her an empty vessel got to hear the story of how God filled it to overflowing.

Emptiness Meets Limitless

I love how God took a woman who's 'Now What?' moment was defined by lack and emptiness and responded by asking her to find even more emptiness. God was not teasing this widow or trying to discourage her, he was about to display his limitless resources as the oil started pouring and the miracle kept coming. God was breaking every restriction she had in her heart and mind as she realised 'this oil will only stop when I limit its flow.'

The limitless God we serve isn't afraid of the emptiness in our lives; you can never bring more jars than God can fill. His resources are endless and in our 'Now What?' moments, he doesn't just want to fulfill our need, but also to change our mindset. Every extra jar that God filled beyond her own changed the widow's perspective about her possibilities to increase and her situation to not just improve, but to completely turnaround.

This widow made a complete turnaround transitioning from lack to plenty and from fear to faith. She navigated a new way to pay her debts from pouring out her oil and she navigated a new path for her boys who would never have to face the same challenges she did. The widow got her spiritual software updated to refresh her thinking about the God that she served and the way in which he worked.

From Trials to Trails

Have you ever been on a walk in the countryside and noticed that alongside the well-worn footpath you are following there are often smaller trails. These paths are less direct but they look far more interesting to travel on. 'Now What?' moments create those unique trails when for various reasons you leave the main footpath and navigate a new way. The route you will create may not be as straightforward, it may require you to journey for longer or even cross some unforeseen rough terrain. But it will give you new climbing skills, expose you to brand new scenery and even introduce you to some new travelling companions on the way.

I pray this book has strengthened you to keep going and create a pathway through your 'Now What?' moments. One day someone might lose their way, their trial might knock them off course causing them to lose connection with all that is familiar. As they journey on through their confusion they may just stumble across the path your 'Now What?' moment carved.

Your trial will become their trail; it will help them find their way home.

Now What?

Tips For Living A Limitless Life

1. Don't let 'Now What?' moments install spiritual speed cameras in your life.

2. God will ask you to look again at your life; be willing to offer whatever you find – it may be the beginning of your miracle.

3. God is a turnaround God so make sure you visit the reclamation yard in your 'Now What?' moment.

4. Your 'Now What?' moments can often be transitional so learn to navigate well.

5. Your trial will become others 'Now What?' trail.

Thank you to those who have determined to push past the pain; to you who have refused to quit; to the one who is persevering in the trial. I add my applause to all of heaven's chorus that is cheering you on.

Your breakthrough is coming – the tears are temporary but the rewards are eternal. Your refusal to quit allows others to succeed and your persistence secures their promise. God is with you and these present trials will become tomorrow's trophies of His grace and goodness.

So thank you for the legacy you are securing, the story you are writing and the path you are carving out. Your 'Now What?' moments will become someone else's welcome wisdom.

Love

Charl

OTHER BOOKS BY CHARLOTTE GAMBILL

CONSUMER OR CONSUMED?
IN HER SHOES
IDENTITY

FOR FURTHER RESOURCES:

For more teaching resources by
Charlotte Gambill please visit
www.charlottegambill.com

Email: info@charlottegambill.com
Twitter.com/charlgambill
Facebook.com/charlgambill